D0108856

The POCKET
ENCYCLOPEDIA
of
IRELAND

GILL BOOKS

The POCKET
ENCYCLOPEDIA
of
IRELAND

Gill Books

Hume Avenue, Park West, Dublin 12

www.gillbooks.ie

Gill Books is an imprint of M.H. Gill & Co.

Copyright © 2012 / 2014 Teapot Press

ISBN: 978-0-7171-5028-1

This book was created and produced by Teapot Press Ltd

Text: Mel Plehov
General Editor: Elizabeth Golding
Design: Alyssa Peacock & Tony Potter
Editors: Mel Plehov, Elizabeth Golding,
Fiona Biggs & Catherine Gough
Consultant Editors: Natasha Mac a'Bhaird & Amanda Bell

Printed in Europe by Factor Druk

This book is typeset in Minion & Dax

A CIP catalogue record for this book is available
from the British Library.

5 4 3

Contents

Introduction

With beautiful landscapes and unspoiled scenery, Ireland is often nicknamed 'The Emerald Isle' because of its idyllic, green panoramas. Bursting with history and tradition, Ireland has a rich and varied past that has not only impacted its own cultural heritage, but, due to emigration, has also impacted many cultures around the world.

As well as the magnificence of the countryside, there are many towns and cities noted for their cultural importance, with reputations for academic excellence, architectural wonders and, of course, fantastic bars!

The entries that follow cover a wealth of information, from Irish history, culture and politics through to towns, tourist attractions and landmarks, as well as information on notable Irish men and women. It has been designed so that all the information you need is at your fingertips, is easily accessible and covers every possible thing you would need to know in a succinct and easy-to-understand way.

The book also contains extended articles on key topics, providing extra detail on important events that affected Irish history and

culture, such as The Great Famine, Religion in Ireland and the Irish Diaspora.

For a quick overview of Irish history, there is an abridged timeline offering a quick glimpse of Ireland's captivating past.

This is the easiest way to uncover the myths, legends, history and attractions that this rich, diverse and enchanting island has to offer. Either start at A, or use the contents and index to find entries of particular interest.

Timeline

1801	Ireland becomes part of the UK
1845	The Great Famine
1870	Home Rule Association set up
1881	Land Acts introduce fair rent and tenancy agreements
1905	Sinn Féin founded
1916	Easter Rising
1918	Sinn Féin victory in General Election
1919	Outbreak of War of Independence; First Dáil meets
1921	War of Independence ends; Anglo-Irish Treaty signed
1923	Civil War
1937	New Irish Constitution adopted; first Taoiseach is Éamon de Valera
1948	Ireland declares itself a republic
1972	Bloody Sunday
1985	Anglo-Irish Agreement
1998	Good Friday Agreement
2002	Currency changes to the euro
2009	Protest in Dublin over the recession
2010	Saville Report into Bloody Sunday is released
2011	Queen Elizabeth II visits Ireland
2015	Ireland becomes the first country to legalise same-sex marriage in a popular vote

A

A, B, C Specials A reserve police force set up in 1920, just before the founding of Northern Ireland. It was set up by the British government to protect Ulster from *IRA* attacks. A Specials were the elite, full-time force, B Specials were part-time and unpaid, and C Specials were a reserve force. The force was made up almost entirely of Protestants. After 1925 the A and C Specials disbanded. 'B men' remained until 1970.

Abbey Theatre A playhouse in Dublin most famous for staging works of famous Irish playwrights, including Lady Gregory, *W. B. Yeats* and Sean O'Casey. It was rebuilt in 1966 by Michael Scott.

Achill Island The largest Irish island, it lies off the coast of *County Mayo.* In 1887 it was connected to the mainland by a bridge.

Act to Provide for the Better Government of Ireland (Government of Ireland Act) *(1920)* The British Parliament passed legislation to divide the island, creating Northern Ireland and what was then Southern Ireland (now the Republic of Ireland), with two separate governments, albeit with very limited powers. This is often referred to as *Partition*.

Act of Union *(1800)* The British government made moves to abolish the Irish parliament after the *Rebellion of 1798,* which was against British rule in Ireland. Through bribery, corruption, patronage and intimidation, the Union came into effect on the first day of 1801 and created the United Kingdom of Great Britain and Ireland, which lasted until the formation of the Irish Constitution in 1922.

ACHILL ISLAND
The current bridge to the mainland was completed in 2008.

PARTITION CARTOON
This political cartoon shows the Ulster pig walking away from the Home Rule pen.

IRISH SHEEP FARM
Eighty per cent of agricultural land is devoted to grass.

Adams, Gerry *(1948–)* Politician and leader of the political party, *Sinn Féin*. Initially a civil rights protester, it is often claimed he has links with the *IRA*; however, he denies such claims. He was instrumental in ending the 1981 *Hunger Strike*. He was elected to the British parliament in 1983, but refused to take an oath of allegiance to the Queen. He was a key figure in the peace negotiations that culminated in the 1994 IRA ceasefire and the *Good Friday Agreement* in 1998.

Aer Lingus Ireland's oldest airline. Established in 1936, it has a European and transatlantic network with 65 destinations served.

Agriculture Irish agricultural land is used for grazing, dairy and arable farming. Irish land produces an excellent grass crop. Beef and dairy products account for 60 per cent of agricultural output. Agriculture used to be the most important industry, but due to industrialisation it now accounts for only 4 per cent of the GDP.

Ahern, Bertie *(1951–)* Politician most famous for his part in the *Good Friday Agreement* of 1998. He became leader of Fianna Fáil in 1994, and was Taoiseach from 1997 to 2007. He resigned from the party in 2012 in the wake of a corruption inquiry

Aikenhead, Mary *(1787–1858)* A Protestant from Cork who converted to Catholicism and became a nun. She set up the Irish Sisters of Charity in 1816, and founded convents, schools, and Our Lady's Hospice for the Dying at Harold's Cross, Dublin.

Alexander, Cecil Frances *(1818–1895)* Poet and hymn-writer most famous for *All Things Bright and Beautiful* and *Once in Royal David's City.*

PEACE TALKS
Meeting with international politicians during the Northern Ireland peace talks.

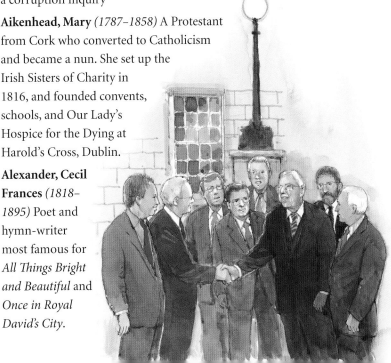

**TRADITIONAL
IRISH DANCERS**
The Irish Dancing
Commission was
founded in 1929.

Allen, Dave *(1936–2005)* Controversial comedian whose material about religion and sex led to him being banned on Australian TV. Despite objections from moralists, he fronted many famous British TV shows in the 1970s.

Allen, Lough A lake (lough) situated in the counties of *Leitrim* and *Roscommon*, in the north of the Republic of Ireland. The river Shannon flows through the lake.

Allgood, Sara *(1883–1950)* An actor who appeared in over 30 Hollywood films, eventually becoming a US citizen in 1945. She appeared in the opening night production of *Spreading the News* at *The Abbey Theatre*.

An Coimisiún le Rincí Gaelacha (The Irish Dancing Commission) Founded in 1929, it controls all aspects of Irish step dancing, including the rules for examinations, competitions and teaching standards.

Anglo-Irish Agreement *(1985)* An agreement confirming the end of the War of Independence. Signed in November between the British and Irish governments, it gave the Republic of Ireland a consulting role in the affairs of Northern Ireland.

Anglo-Irish Treaty *(1921)* An agreement confirming the end of the *Anglo-Irish War*. It endorsed the separation of Northern and Southern Ireland.

Anglo-Irish War *(1919–1921)* referred to in Ireland as the *War of Independence*, it was fought between the *IRA* and British armed forces. It was triggered by the assassination of two British policemen in *Tipperary* by the *IRA*. The Black and Tans' cruel tactics and attacks on Irish civilians undermined British rule. A truce was called in 1921 and peace talks led to the *Anglo-Irish Treaty*.

THE ANGLO-IRISH TREATY
The Anglo-Irish Treaty was signed on 6 December 1921.

THE COAST OF COUNTY ANTRIM
Its coastline boasts many ancient ruins.

An Taibhdhearc (pronounced Tive Yark), is the national Irish language theatre, based in Galway city. It was founded in 1928. It suffered extensive smoke damage during a fire in 2007 and closed for renovation and refurbishment. The theatre re-opened in autumn 2012.

Antrim, County The northernmost county of Northern Ireland. Its main city, and the capital of Northern Ireland, is *Belfast*. Antrim's main features are *The Giant's Causeway, Carrickfergus Castle* and *Lough Neagh*. It has a long coastline of white chalk cliffs and is separated from Scotland by 13 miles (21 km). The land, particularly around the Bann Valley, is important for *agriculture*.

Antrim, town Antrim is a market town now rich with industrial companies, such as engineering and construction businesses. It is the site of the Battle of Antrim where Irish rebels were defeated by British forces in 1798. Antrim was once burned down by Scottish Christians who opposed English forms of worship.

An Túr Gloine (**The Tower of Glass**) An art studio producing stained glass, established in 1903. Glass from the studio can be found in many religious buildings around the world.

Aran Islands A collection of limestone islands off the west coast of Ireland, near *Galway*. The islands are most famous for their preservation of the Irish *language, folklore* and culture that has been passed orally through generations.

Áras an Uachtaráin (President's House) Built in 1751, it is the official residence of the President of Ireland. It is located in Phoenix Park, Dublin.

LANDSCAPE ON INIS MÓR
Irish language and culture is cherished on the Aran Islands.

THE ARDAGH CHALICE
An 8th-century archaeological find from the Early Christian Period.

ANCIENT TOMBS
Newgrange, near Drogheda, is one of the best examples of a passage tomb. It was built in 3200 BC.

Archaeology of Ancient Ireland Archaeology in Ireland has helped date its history back to around 6000–8000 BC. Archaeological finds from ancient Ireland have uncovered many burial sites, one of best known being Newgrange and a burial mound located in *Knocknarea*. Legend has it that Knocknarea contains the remains of an ancient Celtic queen, Medhbh, or Maeve.

Moving further ahead in time, archaeologists later discovered an ancient Irish form of writing called ogham. The discovery of this writing meant historians could pinpoint Ireland's transition from pre-history to history.

With the introduction of Christianity into Ireland in AD 500, the Roman alphabet was introduced; this superseded ogham.

The earliest Christian buildings have not survived, but archaeologists have discovered stone buildings that date back to AD 700, and carbon dating has enabled them to study the way they evolved from simple buildings to great round towers.

Archaeological evidence has also been used to learn about early Irish food, farming, tools for agriculture, pottery, glass, clothing and art.

The study of manuscripts shows how initial carvings on stone slabs evolved into two of Ireland's most famous manuscripts, *The Book of Durrow* and *The Book of Kells*. In fact, archaeological investigation suggests that The Book of Kells began its life in Iona, Scotland, in the 8th century and was merely finished in Kells.

STONE CARVINGS

The carvings in passage tombs, like Newgrange, were made without iron tools. The engineering is so exact that on the shortest day each year, the sun comes through the doorway and lights up the central chamber.

ROUND STONE TOWERS
Monasteries built stone towers with doors 10 ft (3 m) off the ground so that the Vikings could not steal their treasures.

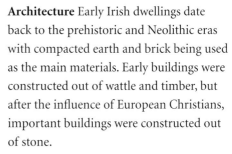

Architecture Early Irish dwellings date back to the prehistoric and Neolithic eras with compacted earth and brick being used as the main materials. Early buildings were constructed out of wattle and timber, but after the influence of European Christians, important buildings were constructed out of stone.

Norman military structures began to influence Irish buildings in the early 13th century, the most famous example of this being Dublin Castle.

Classicism influenced courthouses and military bases during the 1500s; the most notable buildings in the classical style are Parliament House (now the Bank of Ireland) and Trinity College Library, both in Dublin.

During the 1800s, the Georgian influence gave Dublin the look we see today. However, Gothic Revival architecture was later adopted and can be seen, most notably in the cathedrals around the counties of *Cork, Armagh* and *Donegal*.

Domestic architecture quickly changed from the slum housing of the 19th century to houses spread around the outskirts of towns.

Twentieth-century architecture is dominated by Michael Scott, who is responsible for the controversial Dublin Bus terminal, Busáras, as well as the exposed steel structure of the P. J. Carroll factory in *Dundalk*. The Spire of Dublin, or Monument of Light, was built in 2003, as part of a regeneration project on Dublin's O'Connell Street.

KILKENNY CASTLE
An important site first built by the Norman Strongbow in the 12th century, it was the seat of the Butlers of Ormonde for 600 years, and was handed over to the State in 1969.

THE ROYAL HOSPITAL, DUBLIN
A fine example of 17th-century architecture, it now houses the Irish Museum of Modern Art (IMMA).

Ardgillan Castle Built in 1738, it is a large country house in *County Dublin*.

Ardmore Studios Film studios built in 1958 in Bray, County Wicklow.

Armagh, County Lying to the south of Northern Ireland, Armagh has been settled by both the Scots and the English. Its textile industry helped sustain its people through the worst years of *The Great Famine*. Armagh was the home of the kings of Ulster for 700 years and is now the seat of both the Roman Catholic and Protestant archbishops of Ireland.

ARDGILLAN CASTLE
The castle and its gardens are a popular tourist attraction.

Armagh, City Dominated by the Cathedral of St Patrick, Armagh is characterised by its Georgian remodelling of the town during the early 1800s. It is the least-populated city in Northern Ireland.

Art Pottery was one of the first crafts developed in Ireland during the Neolithic Age. In the Iron Age, the *Celts* brought one of the most famous and distinctive art movements to Ireland. Celtic designs incorporated flowing lines, scrolls, trumpet shapes and bird heads.

After the introduction of Christianity, most Irish art was religious and the first notable collectors were Protestant gentry of the 18th century.

The National Gallery opened on Merrion Square in 1864. The Millennium Wing on Clare Street was added in 2002. The National Gallery collection holds some 15,000 works of art. *The Irish Museum of Modern Art (IMMA)* opened in 1991 in the 17th-century Royal Hospital Kilmainham.

THE NATIONAL MUSEUM OF IRELAND

The National Museum of Ireland includes the museum at Collins Barracks, which opened in 1997 and houses collections of the Art and Industry division of the museum's holdings.

Bacon, Francis *(1909–1992)* A famous, self-taught artist renowned for his works depicting the human figure. His studio can be viewed in Dublin City Gallery, the Hugh Lane.

Bale, John *(1495–1563)* English Protestant Bishop of Ossory. His radical views often ostracised him from the local community. When the Catholic Queen Mary acceded to the throne he fled Ireland.

Ballet Although not as popular as Irish traditional dance, ballet is celebrated and there are three professional companies: the Cork City Ballet, the Irish National Youth Ballet and Ballet Ireland.

BALLET
Ballet is a popular form of dance in Ireland.

Banim, John *(1798–1842)* and **Michael** *(1796–1874)* Brothers from *County Kilkenny*, who were both writers. Their work often romanticised the plight of Irish peasants, most notably in *Tales by the O'Hara Family*.

RIVER BANN
The longest river in Northern Ireland.

Bann River Divided into two by *Lough Neagh*. The Upper Bann flows from the Mountains of Mourne. The Lower Bann runs from Lough Neagh to the Atlantic Ocean.

Banshee (Woman of the Fairies) According to Irish *folklore*, a banshee is a female death messenger from a supernatural world. Her cry heralds death and is alleged to follow certain families.

BANTRY HOUSE
The house boasts landscaped gardens and collections of art, furniture and tapestries.

Bantry House Built to look across Bantry Bay, the 18th-century house in County Cork is open to the public.

Barrow River that crosses many Irish counties; it ends its journey at Waterford harbour.

Barry, Tom *(1897–1980)* A Republican revolutionary who commanded *IRA* units during the *War of Independence*. In 1937 he succeeded *Seán Mac Bride* as chief-of-staff of the IRA but resigned following disagreements in 1938.

Battle of Aughrim *(1691)* Often referred to as 'The War of Two Kings', as the conflict was between the Catholic King James II and the would-be King of England, William of Orange, who was Protestant. King James was supported by Jacobites in Ireland, but there was strong opposition from Protestants. The Jacobites were defeated at this battle and there was Protestant rule over Ireland for many years to come.

Battle of Benburb *(1646)* A famous victory for Irish Confederates, who pushed back Scottish forces wanting to conquer Ireland.

Battle of the Boyne *(1690)* A turning point for William of Orange, who defeated King James II's men. The battle is commemorated by the *Orange Order* on 12 July every year.

Battle of Clontarf *(1014)* *Brian Bórú's Munster* forces fought *Viking* armies from *Leinster* on Clontarf beach, killing nearly all of them. Bórú died after the battle, leaving Ireland leaderless, but with the Vikings severely depleted, peace reigned for several years.

BATTLE OF THE BOYNE
A turning point during 'The War of the Two Kings'.

BATTLE OF CLONTARF
It ended with the Irish chasing the Vikings into the sea.

ROSSNOWLAGH BEACH
Ireland has some of the most beautiful, unspoiled coastlines in the world.

Beaches Ireland boasts beautiful landscapes and miles of coastline. Some of the beaches regarded as the best are:

✦ Bundoran Beach (*Donegal*) Best known for the 'Surfing World Championships', but you don't have to surf to enjoy 1.2 miles (2 km) of unspoiled sandy beaches.

✦ Benone Strand (*Derry*) Famous for miles of golden sands with huge sand dunes to explore, and it even has its own protected nature reserve.

✦ Duncannon Beach (*Wexford*) Regarded as one of the best beaches in the south-east and has over 1 mile (1.6 km) of golden sands.

✦ Balbriggan Beach (*Dublin*) A short walk from the town centre, it is home to a large seal colony and is a great site for quiet coastal walks.

✦ Rossnowlagh Beach (*Donegal*) Also known as 'Heavenly Cove', it is one of the most picturesque beaches facing the Atlantic Ocean.

Beckett, Samuel *(1906–1989)* Writer and poet. He studied at Trinity College Dublin and taught briefly in Belfast before taking up a lecturing position in Paris, where his career as a writer began. He was awarded the Nobel Prize for Literature in 1969. His most famous works include: *Waiting for Godot, Malone Dies* and *How It Is.*

SAMUEL BECKETT
An extremely influential writer.

Bective Abbey An ancient Cistercian abbey built in 1147. Rebuilt over the centuries, it eventually became a Tudor mansion before falling into ruin. It was used as a location during the 1995 film *Braveheart.*

Behan, Brendan *(1923–1964)* Famous playwright and poet, he was best known for his work, *Borstal Boy*, which he wrote whilst imprisoned for his participation in the *IRA* bombing campaign in Britain. Behan found dealing with fame difficult and began to drink heavily. He developed diabetes and died at a young age.

BECTIVE ABBEY
The Cistercian abbey in County Meath has been remarkably preserved.

BELFAST CASTLE
One of the county's most famous landmarks.

Belfast Set in the county of *Antrim*, it is the capital city of Northern Ireland. However, due to its low-lying position it was not considered as important in historical times as *Carrickfergus*. Today the town is said to be split in two, with Protestants living in the east and Catholics in the west. It is home to *Stormont*, the seat of the *Northern Ireland Assembly*, Waterfront Hall, Belfast Castle, City Hall, *Queen's University*, the Botanic Gardens and the Ulster Museum.

The shipbuilding industry was established in Belfast in the 18th century, which united local Catholic and Protestant workers; in 1912, the *Titanic* was built in Belfast.

Belfast Lough An inlet on the east coast of Northern Ireland. Its shores reach as far as the cities of *Belfast*, *Carrickfergus* and Bangor.

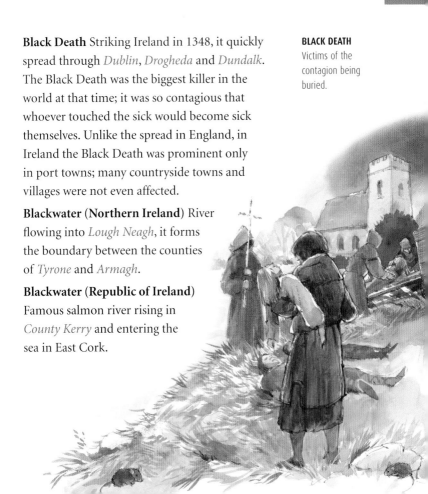

Black Death Striking Ireland in 1348, it quickly spread through *Dublin*, *Drogheda* and *Dundalk*. The Black Death was the biggest killer in the world at that time; it was so contagious that whoever touched the sick would become sick themselves. Unlike the spread in England, in Ireland the Black Death was prominent only in port towns; many countryside towns and villages were not even affected.

Blackwater (Northern Ireland) River flowing into *Lough Neagh*, it forms the boundary between the counties of *Tyrone* and *Armagh*.

Blackwater (Republic of Ireland) Famous salmon river rising in *County Kerry* and entering the sea in East Cork.

BLACK DEATH
Victims of the contagion being buried.

BLARNEY CASTLE
The castle was built as a medieval stronghold.

Blarney Castle Built in 1446 in *County Cork*, the castle is best known for housing the *Blarney Stone*.

Blarney House Georgian manor house built in the grounds of *Blarney Castle* in the 19th century.

Blarney Stone A block of bluestone found within *Blarney Castle*. Legend has it that kissing the Blarney Stone will bring you the gift of 'the blarney', which can be roughly translated as 'the gift of the gab'. To achieve this, first you have to climb to the top of the castle and then lean backwards over the ledge.

Blood's Plot A Protestant conspiracy masterminded by Captain Thomas Blood in 1663. The objective was to seize Dublin Castle and kidnap the Duke of Ormonde. Blood's plot was uncovered, but he escaped arrest and went on to make an assassination attempt on the duke in 1670. He was finally arrested in 1671 whilst trying to steal the English crown jewels.

B

Bloody Sunday *(1972)* The name given to 30 January 1972 when British forces shot dead 13, and wounded 12, unarmed civil rights protesters in *Derry*. The units had been deployed to arrest 'troublemakers' during a peaceful demonstration. An inquiry found the killings to be 'unjustified and unjustifiable'. British Prime Minister David Cameron made a formal apology on behalf of the UK in 2010.

Blount, Charles *(1563–1606)* English soldier who played a key role in completing the Elizabethan conquest of Ireland in 1603.

BLOODY SUNDAY
Civilians and army at the scene of the shootings.

Blueshirts A right-wing movement established in 1932, it grew out of the Army Comrades Association and was made up of mainly rural workers who opposed the Irish government's *Economic War* with Britain. The Blueshirts were led by Eoin O'Duffy. In 1933 they merged with Cumann na nGaedheal to form Fine Gael, and by 1936 the Blueshirts had faded away.

Board of Works A committee set up in 1831 by the British government to help improve the economic and social conditions in Ireland. It made improvements to land navigations and redeveloped roads and bridges, providing transient works during the *Great Famine*. The Board of Works was taken over by the Department of Finance following *Irish Independence* and is now called the Office of Public Works.

Bono *(1960–)* Born Paul David Hewson, he is a singer best known for his involvement with the band *U2*.

BONO
He is well known for his humanitarian efforts.

Book of Common Prayer An Anglican prayer book introduced to Ireland in the 1500s. It was the same as the English book until the Church of Ireland became independent in 1878.

Bórú, Brian *(941–1014)* High King of Ireland from 1002 to 1014 who recaptured *Munster* from the *Vikings*. In 1005 he declared *Armagh* the religious capital of Ireland. In return the Book of Armagh named him Emperor of the Irish. He later defeated the Vikings in the *Battle of Clontarf*, but was killed the same day when he was trampled by fleeing Vikings.

BRIAN BÓRÚ
As a child, he saw his mother murdered by Viking raiders.

Bothy Band Traditional Irish band of the 1970s. They combined traditional Irish instruments with powerful and energetic arrangements. They made their debut at *Trinity College Dublin* in 1975.

Bourke, Brian *(1936–)* Artist famous for his expressionist style. His most famous works include the *Don Quixote Series*.

B

RICHARD BOYLE
An important figure in the
English colonisation of Ireland.

BOYNE RIVER
The site of The Battle
of the Boyne in 1690.

Boyle, Richard *(1566–1643)* 1st Earl of Cork who used his position to defraud the government, his most notable act being the purchase of Sir Walter Raleigh's *Munster* estates for a despicably low price.

Boyle, Robert *(1627–1691)* Son of *Richard Boyle*, Robert became a scientist and was responsible for Boyle's Law relating to gases. Also a philosopher and philanthropist, Boyle funded the translation of the Bible into Irish and Turkish.

Boyle Abbey One of the largest abbeys in Ireland, it dates back to the 12th century. It remains well preserved despite attacks during the Elizabethan and Cromwellian eras.

Boyne River rising in *Kildare* and flowing through *Drogheda* and into the Irish Sea. The *Battle of the Boyne* took place west of Drogheda in 1690.

Boyzone Highly successful boy band that consisted of *Ronan Keating*, *Stephen Gately*, Mikey Graham, Keith Duffy and Shane Lynch. They were put together in 1993 by *Louis Walsh*.

Brady, Liam *(1956–)* Footballer who won 72 caps playing for the Republic of Ireland.

Branagh, Kenneth *(1960–)* Belfast-born actor, director and producer, most famous for his parts in Shakespeare productions. He has directed, acted in and written many Hollywood films.

BOYZONE
The four surviving members. Stephen Gately died in 2009.

HA'PENNY BRIDGE
The most famous
bridge in Dublin.

CARRICK-A-REDE
The bridge is open only
during the summer.

Bridges There are many famous and noteworthy bridges in Ireland, including:

✦ The Ha'penny Bridge (*Dublin*) An early cast-iron pedestrian bridge over the *Liffey*. Built in 1816, it used to be toll levied in the 1800s, but is now free to cross.

✦ Carrick-a-Rede Rope Bridge (*Antrim*) A popular tourist attraction. It is a rope bridge suspended above the sea between two cliff edges.

✦ Salmon Weir Bridge (*Galway*) Built in 1818 over the largest weir in Ireland, the bridge is a perfect place to see salmon heading upriver.

✦ The Foyle Bridge (*Derry*) Built between 1980 and 1984, this is the longest bridge in Ireland and one of the most impressive feats of road engineering in Northern Ireland, built to two-lane dual carriageway standard.

✦ Gamble's Bridge (*Down*) Bridge on the Newry Canal Tow Path, which is part of the National Cycle Network. Known locally as 'Crack Bridge', a reference to the Irish word 'craic', which can loosely be translated as fun or gossip.

Brigid, Saint (c. 452–525) Regarded as 'The Mary of the Irish', she is a patron saint of Ireland who represents women in Christianity. Her feast day is 1 February, which is also an important day of the Celtic year.

Brooke, Sir Basil Stanlake, *1st Viscount Brookeborough (1888–1973)* Unionist politician whose views on Northern Ireland's Catholics was infamously bigoted, disallowing Catholics to join the Unionist Party.

Brosnan, Pierce *(1953–)* Actor born in Navan, Co. Meath. Most famous for his role as James Bond, as well as many other Hollywood film appearances.

Browne, Noël *(1915–1997)* Ambitious politician who campaigned for improvements in public provision of health care. His efforts to improve care and support for mothers and children were quashed by the Catholic Church, which regarded the plans as a threat to 'the sanctity of the family'.

PIERCE BROSNAN
He is well known for his charitable work and has been an ambassador for UNICEF since 2001.

B

Burren, the Exposed limestone plateau in *County Clare* extending as far as the *Aran Islands.* The joints in the pavement provide a unique habitat for rare Irish *flora*. Many rivers disappear through swallow-holes and flow underground before emerging as springs. Hundreds of ancient archaeological sites have been found in this region, including tombs, early churches and high *crosses.*

THE BURREN
One of the largest karst landscapes in Europe.

Butlers of Ormonde Originally named Fitzwalter, the Butler family arrived in Ireland during the Norman invasion. The family became extremely wealthy and powerful, ruling over the area surrounding *Munster* for centuries. They based themselves at Kilkenny Castle.

Byrne, Ed *(1972–)* Stand-up comedian best known for appearing on a variety of UK panel shows. He was one of 54 celebrities who openly opposed the pope's visit to the UK in 2010.

GABRIEL BYRNE
Holding an award given to him at the 2006 Edinburgh International Film Festival.

Byrne, Gabriel *(1950–)* Actor, director, producer, writer and narrator. He has starred in over 35 Hollywood films, including *The Usual Suspects* and *Enemy of the State*. He is known for his active involvement with many charities, and in 2004 was appointed a UNICEF Ireland ambassador.

Byrne, Gay *(1934–)* Radio and TV presenter known best for his chat show, *The Late Late Show,* on *RTÉ,* which he hosted from 1962 to 1999.

C

Cahir Town in the county of *Tipperary*. It is the site of many ancient battles and is reputed to be the original site for the coronation of the Munster kings.

Cahir Castle Situated on an island in the River Suir, it dates back to the 13th century, although it was built up into the fortress visible today during the 15th century.

Callan, Nicholas *(1799–1864)* Catholic priest and inventor. His main claim to fame is being one of the first scientists to use an induction coil. His inventions are now displayed in the National Science Museum in Maynooth.

CAHIR CASTLE
One of the largest castles in Ireland.

CAMOGIE FINALS WINNERS OF THE LAST 10 YEARS

Year	Winner	Runner-up	Score	Attendance
2006	Cork	Tipperary	0-12 vs 0-4	20,685
2007	Wexford	Cork	2-7 vs 1-8	33,154
2008	Cork	Galway	2-10 vs 1-8	18,727
2009	Cork	Kilkenny	0-15 vs 0-7	25,924
2010	Wexford	Galway	1-12 vs 1-10	17,290
2011	Wexford	Galway	2-7 vs 1-8	14,974
2012	Wexford	Cork	3-13 vs 3-06	15,900
2013	Galway	Kilkenny	1-9 vs 0-7	15.063
2014	Cork	Kilkenny	2-12 vs 1-09	12,476
2015	Cork	Galway	1-13 vs 0-9	16,610

* In camogie scoring, the goal score plus points score is added, i.e. in 2002 Cork scored 4 goals (worth 3 points each) and 9 points, making a total of 21 points. Tipperary scored 1 goal (worth 3 points) and 9 points, making a total of 12 points.

Camogie A type of *hurling* played by women. It is played by over 1,000 women throughout Ireland and is organised through the Camogie Association. There are 15 players on each team. Scoring is achieved by getting the ball over or under the H-shaped posts. If it goes over the bar, one point is scored. If it goes under, a goal is scored – worth three points.

C

Carleton, William *(1794–1869)* Novelist from *County Tyrone*, who was educated in *hedge schools*. His works depicted Irish life in the 19th century; his most famous work, *Traits and Stories of the Irish Peasantry,* established his reputation and was praised by *W. B. Yeats*.

Carlow, County The second-smallest county in Ireland, it lies in the province of *Leinster*. The land is flat and fertile, which lends itself to dairy farming. Many castles were erected in County Carlow due to its position on the strategic path to Dublin during the Anglo-Norman invasions.

Carlow, town Situated on the *River Barrow*, it was attacked by *Cromwell* and in the *Rebellion of 1798* and was the scene of many bloody battles. Carlow has the first Catholic cathedral to have been built after Catholic emancipation.

CARLOW CASTLE
Built in the 13th century, it is a national monument.

Carolan, Turlough *(1670–1738)* Harpist and composer. His music appealed to both Irish and Anglo-Irish, with musical themes from traditional folk music, as well as contemporary Italian baroque music. He was blinded by smallpox at the age of 18. Over 200 of his compositions have survived into the modern era.

Carrageen Edible seaweed, red in colour, that grows on the shorelines of the Atlantic Ocean. It has many uses, from a gelling agent in soups and confectionery, to pharmaceuticals, curing leather, cattle feed and soil enrichment.

Carrantuohill The highest mountain in Ireland – it is 3,409 ft (1,039 m) tall. It is situated in *County Kerry* and its peak is topped with a large metal cross that is 16 ft (5 m) tall. The mountain is often climbed; crowding and loose stones have caused safety concerns in recent years.

CARRAGEEN
Edible seaweed,
an Irish delicacy.

CARRANTUOHILL
The highest mountain
in Ireland.

Carrickfergus Seaport town near *Belfast* in the county of *Antrim*. It was an important town from the 14th–17th centuries and was the site of many battles between English and Irish forces. The town's walls, which date back to the 17th century, can still be seen; there is also a statue of William of Orange in the harbour and a historical theme park.

CARRICKFERGUS CASTLE
One of the best-preserved medieval structures in Ireland.

Carrickfergus Castle An important stronghold that controlled traffic in and out of *Ulster*. One of the largest Anglo-Norman castles, it was built in the late 12th century.

Carrick-on-Shannon Port town in the county of *Leitrim*, built on the *River Shannon*.

Carrowkeel A Bronze Age cemetery set on top of limestone ridges in *County Sligo*. The remains of Neolithic huts have been found at the foot of the mountains.

Carrowmore A large Neolithic cemetery found in the south-west of *County Sligo*. Archaeologists have discovered remains from 3000 BC.

Carson, Edward *(1854–1935)* Lawyer and Unionist who became leader of the Irish Unionist MPs at Westminster in 1910.

Casement, Roger *(1864–1916)* Nationalist who was executed for treason, for trying to gain German support for the *Easter Rising*.

Cashel, town An important historic site in the county of *Tipperary*. It contains the remains of many Irish settlements, including a 13th-century monastery and a 15th-century castle.

CASHEL ABBEY
A popular tourist attraction with a rich history.

Cashel, Rock of Also known as St Patrick's Rock, it looms over the town of Cashel. It was the original seat for the kings of Munster and was visited by *St Patrick* in the 5th century. Today, you can find remains of Cormac's Chapel, which still houses a Romanesque fresco, as well as a 10th-century wooden church and the *stone cross* of St Patrick.

Castlebar Town in *County Mayo*, an important stronghold during the *Rebellion of 1798*.

Castle Coole 18th-century neoclassical house in *County Fermanagh*. The estate was owned by the Corry family, but is now a National Trust property.

ROCK OF CASHEL
Legend has it that the Rock of Cashel was formed when St Patrick banished Satan from a cave; the displaced rocks landed in Cashel.

CAVAN
The main street of Cavan Town.

Cattle Acts Legislation passed by the British government in 1663–1681 banning Irish meat imports into England. It was regarded as a deliberate ploy to destroy the Irish economy.

Cavan, County County of the Republic of Ireland in the province of *Ulster*; it borders Northern Ireland. Much of the land is boggy and low-lying. Its high population was greatly diminished during *The Great Famine*.

Cavan, town Market town well known for its hand-blown crystal glass. It has a neoclassical Catholic cathedral, built between 1938 and 1942 and dedicated in 1947.

Celts The Celts arrived in Ireland around 500 BC. Many historians believe that the Celts who arrived in Ireland were dispersed from their European lands after Roman invasions. The most famous Celtic sites that have been discovered are: Navan Fort in *County Armagh*, Dún Ailinne in *County Kildare* and the Hill of Tara in *County Meath*.

The law of the Celts was called Brehon Law; people under Brehon Law were defined by the Celtic kingdom in which they lived. Celtic art greatly influenced Irish culture and some of the most famous works, such as the *Book of Kells* and *Celtic High Crosses,* were a product of Celtic Christianity.

CELTS
Families, not individuals, owned land, and wealth was determined by how many cattle you had.

Celtic Tiger Term used to describe the period of rapid economic growth in Ireland in the late 1990s where low inflation, diminishing unemployment and budgetary surplus led to Ireland leading the European Union in economic circles.

Chichester, Arthur *(1563–1625)* English soldier and administrator who was appointed governor of Carrickfergus in 1598. In his early years he fought ruthlessly against Irish rebels. He is well known for his role in the *Plantation of Ulster*. Whilst anti-Catholic, Chichester looked after the 'deserving' indigenous people of *Ulster*.

ERSKINE CHILDERS
He used his yacht to smuggle guns for the Irish Volunteers.

Chieftains Traditional Irish band who played a big part in the revival of Irish folk music during the 1960s.

Childers, (Robert) Erskine *(1870–1922)* English-born Irish Republican who opposed the *Anglo-Irish Treaty*. Childers was executed by firing squad during the *Civil War*.

CITIES OF IRELAND

Named	City status gained	Jurisiction	Population
Dublin	1172	Republic of Ireland	1,110,627
Cork	1185	Republic of Ireland	198,582
Limerick	1199	Republic of Ireland	91,454
Waterford	1206	Republic of Ireland	51,519
Kilkenny	1383	Republic of Ireland	24,423
Derry/Londonderry*	1604	Northern Ireland	83,699
Belfast	1888	Northern Ireland	276,459
Galway	1985	Republic of Ireland	76,778
Armagh	1994	Northern Ireland	14,590
Newry	2002	Northern Ireland	27,433
Lisburn	2002	Northern Ireland	71,465

Civil War *(1922–1923)*
The conflict that followed
the *Anglo-Irish Treaty* in
which the *IRA* declared their
independence from political
control. This culminated in the
Irish government, led by *Michael
Collins*, attacking the headquarters
of the anti-treaty rebels.

DUBLIN
The capital city of the Republic of Ireland.

* Derry gained city status in 1604, but wasn't renamed until 1613

C

Clare, County Situated on the west coast of the Republic of Ireland in the province of *Munster*. It has a reputation for continuing the tradition of Irish *music*. The *Burren*, a unique limestone landscape, lies in the north-west corner of the county.

COUNTY CLARE
The Cliffs of Moher face the Atlantic Ocean.

Clarke, Harry *(1889–1931)* Stained-glass artist and designer. His work is typically in the Art Nouveau style and can be seen in the Honan College Chapel in *Cork* as well as the Dublin City Gallery, *the Hugh Lane*.

Clerke, Agnes Mary *(1842–1907)* Astronomer and writer. She was one of only four women to be elected as an honorary member of the Royal Astronomical Society. Her most famous work, *A Popular History of Astronomy during the Nineteenth Century,* was considered a masterpiece internationally.

MICHAEL COLLINS
Considered the Easter
Rising a bitter failure.

Clonmacnoise An important ancient monastery built in the 6th century. It was raided many times by the *Vikings*, but many of the ruins are still preserved today.

Coffey, Brian *(1905–1995)* A poet who became close friends with *Samuel Beckett*.

Collins, Michael *(1890–1922)* Founding father of Irish independence; *Sinn Féin* leader and Irish Nationalist, he was the founder of the *Irish Republican Army (IRA)*. After the *Anglo-Irish Treaty* he became a minister in the provisional government of the Irish Free State (later known as the Republic of Ireland). He was briefly head of the *Irish Free State* before he was killed by Irish Republicans, who opposed the Treaty.

Collins, Steven *(1964–)* Boxer who has won 36 professional fights, the most notable being against Chris Eubank in 1995.

Colum, Pádraic *(1881–1972)* Writer associated with founding the *Abbey Theatre*.

Colum Cille *(521–597)* Abbot who founded the monastery at Iona, Scotland, after being excommunicated from the Irish church. He is known now as St Columba and his feast day is 9 June.

Comeragh Mountains Mountain range popular for climbing situated in the county of *Waterford*.

Connacht Western province of the Republic of Ireland, which includes the counties of *Mayo*, *Leitrim*, *Galway*, *Roscommon* and *Sligo*. It is the smallest of the four Irish provinces and also has the smallest population.

Connaughton, Shane *(1941–)* Screenwriter and novelist from Kingscourt, Co. Cavan whose work displays local knowledge of the *Troubles* in Northern Ireland.

COLUM CILLE
The patron saint of poets.

CONNEMARA
The area is rich in
megalithic tombs.

JAMES CONNOLLY
Played a leading role
in the Easter Rising.

Connemara Rocky coastline in the north of *County Galway*. It is known for its quarries of green marble. There is a large Irish-speaking community in Connemara. The national park and mountain range is home to many rare and unique *flora*.

Connolly, James *(1868–1916)* A revolutionary who helped form the Irish Citizen Army. He was one of the leaders of the 1916 *Easter Rising*, for which he was executed by the British government.

Constitution *(1937)* A replacement devised by *Éamon de Valera* for the 1922 constitution made after the *Anglo-Irish Treaty*. It removed unpopular links with British rule and claimed sovereignty over Northern Ireland. Many parts of the constitution have been amended, particularly the ban on divorce, as well as removing recognition of the 'special position' of the Catholic Church and removing the claim of ownership over Northern Ireland.

Continuity IRA An extremist terrorist group, originally part of the *IRA* until 1995.

Cork, County The largest county in the Republic of Ireland, situated in the province of *Munster*. It features many popular coastal locations, such as Bantry Bay, and tourist attractions that include *Blarney Castle*.

Cork, City The third-largest city in Ireland, Cork is an important trading centre. Cork has its own university as well as many colleges, museums and art galleries. It is built on an island formed by two branches of the *River Lee*. Cork has many interesting architectural features, including several 18th-century buildings and Gothic Revival churches. Cork hosts one of Europe's biggest jazz festivals every year in late October and has featured the likes of Ella Fitzgerald, Gerry Mulligan and Dave Brubeck in the past.

CORK
The city lights over the River Lee.

COUNTY CORK
A popular rural tourist attraction.

Cormac Mac Airt King of Ireland during the 3rd century. He is said to have taken the crown from the existing king due to his superior wisdom and judgment.

Corrib, Lough Lake in *County Galway*. It contains over 300 islands and is connected to another lake, Lough Mask, through an underground river.

Corrs, The Pop band made up of four siblings from *Dundalk*. They combine pop music with traditional *Irish Music*.

Cosgrave, Liam *(1920–)* Irish politician who was *Taoiseach* from 1973–77. He was leader of the *Fine Gael* party. He became unpopular after making deals with the British government.

Cosgrave, William *(1880–1965)* Politician and leader of the Irish Free State. He was a founding member of *Sinn Féin*, and fought during the *Easter Rising*. He was a supporter of the *Anglo-Irish Treaty*.

WILLIAM COSGRAVE
He took over leadership of the Irish Free State.

Costello, John *(1891–1976)* Twice *Taoiseach* who instigated the withdrawal of Ireland from the Commonwealth and the declaration of the Republic of Ireland.

JOHN COSTELLO
Responsible for the Republic of Ireland Act.

Counter-Reformation The term given to the survival of Irish Catholicism during the establishment of the Church of Ireland.

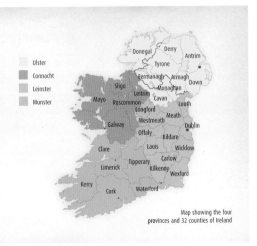

COUNTIES

Irish counties stem from the old Norman and even pre-Norman areas of control. Northern Ireland is made up of six counties in the province of Ulster. The Republic of Ireland is split into 26 counties in all four provinces.

Ulster
Connacht
Leinster
Munster

Donegal · Derry · Antrim
Tyrone
Fermanagh · Armagh · Down
Sligo · Monaghan
Mayo · Leitrim
Roscommon · Cavan
Longford · Louth
Galway · Westmeath · Meath
Offaly · Dublin
Kildare
Clare · Laois · Wicklow
Tipperary · Carlow
Limerick · Kilkenny · Wexford
Kerry · Waterford
Cork

Map showing the four provinces and 32 counties of Ireland

Courcy, John de *(1160–1219)* A Norman prince of *Ulster* during the 12th century, he fell out of favour with the British king and lost his estate.

Croagh Patrick A mountain in *County Mayo* that is considered to be holy as it was the place *St Patrick* went to fast for 40 days during Lent. It is now a place of pilgrimage.

Croke, Thomas *(1824–1902)* Archbishop of *Cashel* and co-founder of the *Gaelic Athletic Association (GAA)*; *Croke Park* in *Dublin* is named after him.

Croke Park Principal stadium and headquarters of the *GAA*. The scene of a massacre on *Bloody Sunday* in 1920. The 4th largest stadium in Europe.

Cromwell, Oliver *(1599–1658)* Leader of England who rampaged through Ireland in 1649 intending to reconquer the country. He sought revenge on all Irish Catholics for the poor treatment of Protestant settlers in 1641. He confiscated land owned by Catholics and created a shift of political power in favour of Protestants.

CROAGH PATRICK
A statue of St Patrick stands at the foot of the mountain.

Crosses, High Intricately carved stone crosses that date back to the time of the *Celts*. Characterized by a circle around the cross, which symbolises the sun. They were often decorated with biblical scenes and were most likely used for religious rituals and decoration, education or marking territories. During the Celtic Revival period, the crosses became popular as gravestone monuments – the tradition remains to this day and has spread throughout the world. The Celtic cross is often used today as a symbol of Ireland and can be found on tourist merchandise, memorabilia and tattoos. The *Gaelic Athletic Association (GAA)* and the Northern Ireland football team use versions of the cross in their logos.

Cú Chulainn A hero of Irish *Mythology*; a brave, invincible warrior with supernatural powers. Like many mythical heroes, he achieved great things at a young age and died a tragic, yet heroic, death.

HIGH CROSSES
Can be found throughout Ireland.

CÚ CHULAINN
A sculpture of the dying Cú Chulainn at the GPO in Dublin.

Cumann na mBan (**The League of Women**) Women's division of the *Irish Volunteers*, founded in 1913. It supported the *Easter Rising* and opposed the *Anglo-Irish Treaty*. Its members went on to serve in the *IRA*; the organization was banned in 1923.

Cumann na nGaedheal (Fine Gael) Political party founded in 1923, see *Fine Gael*.

Curragh, the An open plain of land spanning around 5,000 acres (20 sq km) in *County Kildare*. The area is well known for horse breeding and training, and is home to The Curragh Racecourse.

CURRAGH RACECOURSE
Horses have raced here for centuries.

Curragh Mutiny Also known as the Curragh Incident of 20 March 1914. Sixty British troops based at the Curragh camp chose to resign rather than enforce *home rule* in Ulster. This act discredited the Liberal government in Britain, empowering Unionists and making Nationalists think they had no support from British forces.

Cusack, Cyril *(1910–1993)* Actor involved with the *Abbey Theatre*. He is also known for his many roles with the Royal Shakespeare Company, and a number of small parts in Hollywood films.

Cusack, Michael *(1847–1906)* A teacher from *County Clare* who co-founded the *Gaelic Athletic Association*. The Cusack Stand in *Croke Park* is named after him. He appears in *Ulysses* as 'the Citizen'.

MICHAEL CUSACK
He co-founded the Gaelic Athletic Association (GAA).

D

THE FIRST DÁIL
Met in Dublin in 1919.

Dáil Éireann Lower house of the Irish parliament.

Declaration of 1640 The earliest known claim of Irish independence from British rule. The purpose of the declaration meant that the British no longer had the authority to take people out of Ireland to answer treason charges. The declaration was, in the end, more about the Duke of York covering his own back than a step forward for Irish independence.

Deepwell 19th-century house overlooking Dublin Bay. Its landscaped garden is now a popular tourist attraction.

Defenders A Catholic secret society. Originally a protest group, they fought Protestants in the Battle of the Diamond, after which the Protestants formed the *Orange Order*. They became allies with the *United Irishmen* during the *Rebellion of 1798*.

MANY IRISH
Catholics who joined the Defenders were farmers, living off the land.

Derg, Lough Situated on the *River Shannon,* it is the third-largest lake in the Republic of Ireland. It functions as a reservoir supplying Ardnacrusha power station with water for generating hydroelectricity.

Derg, Lough A much smaller lake in *County Donegal*. One of its islands, Station Island, is a place of pilgrimage, as it is supposed to be the site of *St Patrick's* purgatory, where God showed him a cave that was an entrance to hell. The pilgrimage season lasts between April and September each year.

THE GUILDHALL
Where the Derry
City Council meets.

DERRY
The city lies on the banks
of the River Foyle.

Derry (Londonderry), County County of Northern Ireland. Although Londonderry is its official name, most locals refer to it as Derry. In the past the name Derry was preferred by Nationalists and was used throughout Northern Ireland's Catholic community. 'London' was added to the name in 1613 by King James I and is still preferred by a small minority of Protestants and Unionists. Derry boasts Ireland's longest beach and its economy relies greatly on *agriculture* and *tourism*.

Derry (Londonderry), City The second-largest city in Northern Ireland after *Belfast*. The old city lies to the west of the River Foyle, although the city now spans both banks; the Craigavon Bridge connects new parts of the city to the old parts. Derry will be the UK's first City of Culture in 2013, beating competition from Birmingham, Sheffield and Norwich.

de Valera, Éamon *(1882–1975)* Born in New York and educated in *County Limerick*, he was First President of the Executive Council, and was leader of *Sinn Féin* until he formed a new political party, *Fianna Fáil*. He opposed the Anglo-Irish Treaty; however, while in power he built a relationship with Britain and achieved greater sovereignty over Northern Ireland. He was instrumental in the 1937 Constitution.

de Valois, Ninette *(1898–2001)* Ballet dancer who was instrumental in developing dance schools in Ireland.

Devlin, Anne *(1778–1851)* Servant of revolutionary leader *Robert Emmet*. She carried messages for him, but was arrested and imprisoned for three years.

Devlin, Joseph *(1871–1934)* A leading organizer of the *Irish Volunteers,* he was offered the leadership of the Irish Nationalist Party on Redmond's death in 1918, but conceded the honour to John Dillon.

ÉAMON DE VALERA
The first Taoiseach elected under the Constitution of 1937.

D

Diaspora The term used to describe the great numbers of men and women who have emigrated from Ireland. Most people emigrated to North America, with others moving to Britain, Canada and Australia, as well as other parts of the world. The majority emigrated between 1815 and 1914, and although now living in different countries, the Protestants and Catholics/Unionists and Nationalists took their differences with them. The most notable occurrences of this were the 'Orange and Green' riots that took place in Liverpool and New York.

EMIGRATION
Over 4.5 million people emigrated between 1845 and 1921.

The diaspora meant that Irish politics gained more international coverage than that of other small countries. Irish-Americans became involved in Irish politics, with political parties calling on support and fundraising from Irish communities abroad.

The dispersal of the population meant that Irish culture was introduced to other countries, in the form of *music*, *literature*, drama and dancing. The Irish also passed on the great tradition of *St Patrick's Day*, which is now celebrated in countries throughout the world.

DINGLE PENINSULA
The westernmost
point of Ireland.

Dillon, Gerard *(1916–1971)* Artist whose works have appeared at the Guggenheim, *National Gallery of Ireland* and Pittsburgh International Exhibition. He had a strong association with Roundstone Village in *Connemara*.

Dingle Also known as *An Daingean*. The most westerly town in Europe, situated in *County Kerry*. It is a popular tourist destination and the waters are excellent for fishing. The areas surrounding Dingle are rich in history and contain ancient ruins from the Bronze and Iron Ages, including stone huts and monoliths with carved ogham characters.

Disestablishment *(1869)* The term used to refer to the separation of the Church of Ireland from the state.

Doherty, Ken *(1969–)* Snooker player. He won the World Championship in 1997, beating Stephen Hendry 18-12. In 2011 he reached the semi-finals of the Australian Open; he regularly commentates on matches for the BBC.

Donegal, County County in the Republic of Ireland that borders Northern Ireland. Although the land is barren due to severe weather, Donegal is said to have some of Ireland's most popular *beaches*. Donegal is famous for its sandy beaches and the Glenveagh National Park. It is a bastion of the Irish language. One of Ireland's famous pilgrimages takes place at *Station Island*, situated in *Lough Derg*.

DONEGAL
The county is famous for its idyllic beaches.

D

LEGANANNY DOLMEN
One of Ireland's most
famous megaliths, located
in County Down.

THE GRAVE OF ST PATRICK
He is believed to be buried
in Downpatrick.

Down, County Situated in south-eastern Northern Ireland, it is made up of lowlands and rocky coastline. It features many ancient remains, some even prehistoric. The most famous is Grey Abbey, a 12th-century monastery, and Legananny Dolmen, a Stone Age *megalith*. The main economic output is agricultural, as the land is good for crops and dairy farming. County Down is also home to the Ulster Folk and Transport Museum, which can be found in the town of Holywood.

Downpatrick The largest town in *County Down*. It is said to be the place where *St Patrick* founded his first church. It is also believed that St Patrick is buried nearby, although there is no proof of this. The town lies just south of the city of *Belfast* and many of its residents commute to Belfast for work. The name comes from the Irish 'Dún Pádraig', meaning 'Patrick's stronghold'.

Doyle, Roddy *(1958–)* Novelist most famous for *Paddy Clarke Ha Ha Ha*, which won the Booker Prize in 1993.

Drew, Ronnie *(1934–2008)* Musician and singer who played Irish folk music with *The Dubliners*. He was best known for his distinctive long beard and gravelly voice.

Drogheda Town in *County Louth* which is the last bridging point in the Boyne before it enters the sea.It was the site of *Cromwell*'s siege in 1649 and the *Battle of the Boyne* in 1690. In recent years it has become popular due to rising living costs in Dublin and a good transport and communications infrastructure. The town has a community of independent artists and musicians.

Drury, Susanna *(c.1698–1770)* Celebrated artist who depicted famous Irish landscapes, including *The Giant's Causeway*. She was the first female artist to receive recognition from the Dublin Society.

DROGHEDA
The coat of arms denoting Drogheda as an important port.

THE SPIRE
The centrepiece of
Dublin's regeneration.

Dublin, County County of the *Republic of Ireland* dominated by the capital city of *Dublin*. It also boasts large areas of unspoiled land and sandy beaches.

Dublin, City It gets its name from the Irish 'dubh linn', meaning 'black pool'. It was originally a *Viking* settlement. It became Ireland's main city following the Norman invasion and was, at one stage, one of the largest cities in the British Empire. After the *Partition of Ireland*, it became the capital of the *Irish Free State* (later known as the *Republic of Ireland*).

Georgian architecture is one of the main features of the streets of Dublin and of many important buildings, such as City Hall, the Bank of Ireland, Leinster House (where the parliament sits), the National Library, the Four Courts and the National Museum. Other notable buildings are *Trinity College*, whose library contains the *Book of Kells* and the

Book of Durrow, and Dublin Castle, which was built in the 13th century.

Economic growth, particularly during the *Celtic Tiger* years, helped Dublin regenerate old parts of the city and impressive new buildings emerged. The most iconic landmark is the Spire of Dublin, erected in 2003. It is a huge stainless steel monument situated on O'Connell Street. It stands on the former site of an *IRA* bombing attack that destroyed Nelson's Pillar.

Dublin is famous for its nightlife. The Temple Bar area of the town, the scene of many stag and hen parties, is the cultural quarter of the city and known for its independent shops and bars, although many now regard it as being aimed solely at tourists.

DUBLIN CASTLE
The only surviving original tower.

TEMPLE BAR
The 17th-century street layout has been preserved.

Dubliners, The Band featuring folk singer *Ronnie Drew*. They were popular throughout Ireland and sang politically relevant street-style ballads.

Dún Aengus An ancient ruin of a stone fort situated on one of the *Aran Islands*. It dates back to the Bronze Age.

DUNGUAIRE CASTLE
Tower house on the south-eastern shore of Galway Bay.

Dundalk Town in *County Louth*. It features a Norman castle dating back to the 12th century. Due to its location, it was the scene of many battles over *The English Pale*.

Dunguaire Castle A 16th-century tower house in *County Galway*. Legend has it that if a person asks a question at the gate of the tower, they will find the answer by the end of the day.

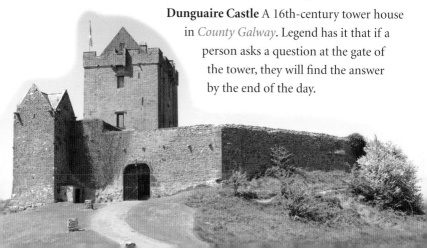

D

Dún Laoghaire A major port in *County Dublin*. It was previously named Kingstown after a visit from George IV in 1821, but was changed in 1921. Its coastal location made it popular with workers from Dublin who chose to live by the sea and commute to the city.

Dunwoody, Richard Jockey who has won over 1,000 races in the UK and Republic of Ireland.

Durcan, Paul *(1944–)* Award-winning poet who is well known for his autobiographical poetry. His work was influenced by the American 'Beat' movement.

Durrow, Book of Famous illuminated manuscript containing the four Gospels. Associated with *Colum Cille*, it is said to have been kept at his monastery in Iona for some time. It now lies in *Trinity College* Library, in *Dublin*.

BOOK OF DURROW
When Durrow Abbey was dissolved, the book went into private ownership before being given to Trinity College Library.

Earhart, Amelia *(1897–1937)* American aviator; she was the first woman to complete a solo transatlantic flight. There is a small museum close to her landing site in *Derry*.

Easter Rising *(1916)* A period of rebellion that began during the Easter weekend. The *Irish Volunteers* became radicalised by the Irish Republican Brotherhood, who were plotting rebellion against British rule in Ireland. They soon joined forces with *James Connolly's Irish Citizen Army*. The rebels lacked firepower, so they negotiated deals with Britain's enemy, Germany. The weapons never reached the rebels, as the German ship was intercepted by the British Navy.

AMELIA EARHART
The first woman to fly transatlantic solo.

On Easter Monday, 24 April, 1,200 rebels met in Dublin and seized control of major buildings, the most famous being the General Post Office. However, they were no match for the heavily armed British forces and the rebellion was called off by 29 April; the main conspirators were condemned to death. Intitially, the rebellion did not have the support of the general population, but as the executions were carried out, public opinion shifted in favour of the rebels.

THE GENERAL POST OFFICE
It still stands today in O'Connell Street.

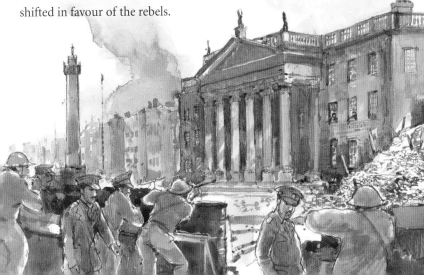

Economics Much of Ireland's economy since the 13th century has been based around *agriculture*. During the 14th century, wool became Ireland's most valuable export and it was marketed as far afield as the Mediterranean and the Middle East.

Thanks to miles and miles of coastline, both on the Atlantic Ocean and Irish Sea, fishing contributed greatly to the prosperity of coastal areas.

During the 17th century, the economy was seriously affected due to political struggles, particularly the rebellion of 1641, and English colonisation.

The Irish economy grew due to cheap labour costs and industrial output of linen and shipbuilding during the Industrial Revolution. In the 1930s, Ireland's economy was severely affected by its *economic war* with Britain. This resulted in the nationalisation of many private industries.

THE IRISH ECONOMY
Grew in strength in the 1960s and again in the 1990s.

After a boom in the 1960s, Ireland's economy struggled during the 1970s due to the *Troubles* in Northern Ireland, inflation, the oil crisis and poor tax management. The 1980s saw high unemployment, overvalued currency and tax rates of up to 60 per cent.

By the 1990s the EU had poured over €10 billion into Ireland's infrastructure. Low corporate tax and a 'social partnership' approach to industry transformed the economy – this period of time became known as the *Celtic Tiger*. Ireland became one of the world's richest nations with low unemployment and income up to 50 per cent higher than in the 1980s.

The Celtic Tiger years were marked by low tax rates, widely available credit and rising house prices. Due to the global financial crisis in 2007, combined with the collapse of the property bubble and banking scandals, Ireland fell into a recession in 2008. This led to an €85 billion bailout in 2010, with big political repercussions.

THE CELTIC TIGER
Low tax and unregulated lending during these years may have led to Ireland's financial collapse.

ÉAMON DE VALERA
He revoked annuities Irish farmers were paying to Britain, which was one of the major catalysts of the war.

Economic War The adoption of mutual trade restrictions between Britain and the Irish Free State during the 1930s. It started with the Irish government retaining annuities paid by farmers who had received loans from Britain to buy their land. Britain responded by imposing charges on imports to the UK. Many farmers lost out, with some forming the *Blueshirts* organisation in response.

As well as retaining the annuities, the Irish Free State abolished its oath of fidelity to the British Empire. Although many farmers lost out and had to pay more money to the Irish government, the willingness of *Éamon de Valera* and his *Fianna Fáil* political party to take a confrontational stance against Britain increased his, and the party's, popularity.

The war came to an end with the 1938 *Anglo-Irish Trade Agreement* when Britain dropped its claim for the annuities and settled for a final pay-off of £10 million.

MARIA EDGEWORTH
A firm believer in
education for women.

RICHARD EDGEWORTH
Despite being English, he
voted against the Act of Union.

Edgeworth, Maria *(1767–1849)* Novelist who campaigned for women's education. Although she was born in England, much of her life was spent in *County Longford*. Her novels were predominantly about Anglo-Irish country society and through the stories she aimed to instill responsibility for Irish peasants in the Anglo-Irish landlords. Her writing was characterised by humour, character studies and social reflections. Her work inspired Scottish novelist Walter Scott, with whom she became friends.

Edgeworth, Richard *(1744–1817)* Anglo-Irish politician, writer and inventor. His most famous invention is the perambulator, a land-measuring wheel. He was a landlord in *County Longford* who was concerned with improvements to his estate and aimed to be a role model for other Anglo-Irish landlords. He edited pro-Union messages into the novels of his daughter, *Maria Edgeworth*.

E

Education From the late 17th century, Catholics were forbidden to set up schools or to send their children to school, so a system of *hedge schools* developed. In 1831 the Board of Education set up the national school system. These schools largely remain under diocesan patronage. Alternatives are provided by Gaelscoileanna, multidenominational schools, or independent fee-paying primary schools. In 1967 free secondary education was introduced. The choice of secondary schools includes voluntary schools, which are run by religious communities or private organizations. Trinity College was established in 1592 and was Protestant dominated until 1970. In 1845 Queen Victoria founded colleges in Belfast, Cork and Galway. In 1854 the Catholic University of Ireland was founded; it became University College Dublin in 1882. In 1908 the Irish Universities Act created the National University of Ireland and a separate Queen's University Belfast. Dublin City University and the University of Limerick were given university status in 1989.

QUEEN'S UNIVERSITY
Over 20,000 students study here each year.

Éire The Irish name for the Republic of Ireland; adopted in 1937 as part of the *Irish Constitution*.

EEC the European Economic Community, which the Republic of Ireland joined in 1973, was set up to facilitate European economic integration. Sometimes referred to as the Common Market, it is now known as the EU (European Union).

EU FLAG
The circle of stars on a blue background represents completeness and unity.

Electoral System (Republic of Ireland) The Irish government consists of a senate, called the *Seanad,* and a lower house, called the *Dáil*.

Members of the Dáil are elected candidates who represent their constituencies. When voting, a proportional representation system is used, rather than the British first-past-the-post system. With proportional voting voters mark more than one choice on the ballot slips. This means that if their first choice candidate does not reach the required quota, their vote goes to their next preferred candidate, and so on. The system allows smaller political parties to win seats.

ROBERT EMMET
Was an active member of the United Irishmen.

ENNISKILLEN CASTLE
Was rebuilt in the 17th century.

Emergency, the The term given to the Second World War period when Ireland remained neutral.

Emmet, Robert *(1778–1803)* Nationalist who was heavily involved in the *Rebellion of 1798*. He went on to lead an unsuccessful revolt in 1803 and was executed for treason.

Ennis, town Town in *County Clare*. Its economy is heavily reliant on manufacturing. Outside the courthouse is a statue of former *Taoiseach* and president, *Éamon de Valera*, who represented the county in general elections.

Enniskillen Market town in *County Fermanagh*; it is well known for being the site of an *IRA* attack on Remembrance Day in 1987.

Enniskillen Castle 15th-century castle on the River Erne that was once connected to the town only via a drawbridge.

Environment Ireland's environment is
a product of high annual rainfall and
prevailing south-west winds from the
Atlantic. Air pollution is low and the rivers
and lakes are of a high standard. The low
population density over much of the country
has helped to preserve the quality of the
landscape. The protection of the environment
is a major objective of government, as a clean
environment is recognised as a key economic
factor. The environment is particularly
relevant to the tourism, agriculture and food
production industries, as well as other natural
resource-based industries. The Environmental
Protection Agency promotes and implements
standards for environmental protection and
management. Since the 1960s, industry has
resulted in major urban development and
changed farming methods, although, much
of Ireland's landscape remains unspoiled.
Ireland is often called the Emerald Isle,
due to its green landscape.

THE EMERALD ISLE
Ireland's nickname, due to its
unspoiled, green landscape.

E

ENYA
Her most famous single,
'Orinoco Flow (Sail Away)',
reached number one in many
countries, including the UK.

Enya *(1961–)* Stage name of Eithne Ní Bhraonáin. She first performed with the folk group Clannad before forging a successful solo career as a singer and songwriter – her most famous album was *Watermark*, released in 1988.

Erne, Lough Lake in *County Fermanagh*; it has two sections that are linked by the River Erne. Many of its islands contain ancient relics.

Ervine, St John *(1883–1971)* Playwright and novelist who managed *The Abbey Theatre*. He fell out of favour with the theatre after the *Easter Rising* of 1916 because of his lack of support for Republican ideals.

Essex, Robert Devereux *(1565–1601)* 2nd Earl of Essex, he led British forces against the Irish. However, he was suspected of sympathising with nationalists when he failed to fight, called a truce and attended secret meetings. He was beheaded for treason.

Essex, Walter Devereux *(1541–1576)* 1st Earl of Essex, helped to suppress Irish rebellion against British rule and masterminded a failed recapturing of *Ulster* in 1575.

Euro The Republic of Ireland changed its currency in 2002 from the *punt* to the euro. The change coincided with an economic boom, which caused high inflation.

Eurovision European song contest in which Ireland has been particularly successful. In 1994 Ireland hosted the contest and introduced the world to the now famous dance show, *Riverdance*.

EURO
Ireland changed its currency in 2002.

Famine, The Great A terrible time in Irish history between 1845 and 1852 when the repeated failure of the potato crop led to widespread famine. Potato consumption in Ireland was huge; it was the staple food for the majority of people, as well as providing fodder for pigs.

The famine was caused by a severe outbreak of *potato blight*, which had been transported to Ireland from Europe and North America via imported fertilizers. Potato blight causes the crop to rot whilst in the ground, making it inedible.

Initially, the British government dealt with it by importing maize into the country.

POTATO CROPS
Were affected by blight and were inedible.

However, later administrations saw the famine as the responsibility of Irish landlords, who failed to provide adequate help for their tenants. Most churches considered the famine to be a punishment from God, so they regarded those who were suffering and starving as sinners.

THE WORKHOUSES
Were a last resort, but even so could help only 20 per cent of the people affected.

The number of pigs fell by over two-thirds and workhouses became overcrowded and disease-ridden due to a massive influx of starving peasants. The death toll began to rise, with many being buried in mass graves, or simply left to rot because many feared they would contract diseases if the dead bodies were touched. Due to overcrowding, contagious diseases such as typhoid, dysentery and fevers became rampant.

Massive emigration followed, with many Irish landlords paying for tenants to be shipped to America or Britain.

FAMINE SHIPS
Between 1847 and 1853, 53 boats were lost at sea (because they were not seaworthy in the first place) and over 9,000 people died from disease or drowning.

Famine Ships Impoverished tenants in Ireland who relied on the potato crop could no longer afford to live. Irish landlords saw an easy solution to this and simply paid for them to emigrate. Families were promised food and money before being packed onto ships for up to three months. The ships became known as coffin ships due to sick and dying passengers passing on disease to healthy passengers. Many of the dead were thrown overboard. When the emigrants arrived at their destination, the promises of food and money turned out to be false, and homeless, penniless exiles were left on the shore to make their own way.

Farrell, Colin *(1976–)* Award-winning Dublin-born actor. He has appeared in many famous Hollywood films, and UK and US TV shows.

Fastnet Rock A large rock formation off the coast of *County Cork*. It features a lighthouse visible from 18 miles (29 km) away and is a point in the annual Round Ireland Yacht Race.

DEER
Three species live
in Ireland today.

VIVIPAROUS LIZARD
Lives further north than
any other reptile.

Fauna Ireland is home to many species of mammals, reptiles, amphibians and fish, though only 26 land mammal species are native, others having arrived here when access was still possible by land bridge from Europe. Species now extinct include the Irish elk, wolf and bear. Four hundred bird species have been recorded. Ireland's only land reptile is the viviparous lizard; this can be found most commonly in the mountains and in national parks. There are also common European frogs, toads and newts; the frog is said to have been introduced from Britain in the 1700s.

The only native freshwater fish in Irish waters are those that can also survive in salt water, such as salmon and trout. Other freshwater fish were introduced during the 1500s.

William Thompson's book, *The Natural History of Ireland*, published in 1849, is still the most comprehensive guide to Irish fauna.

Fenian Movement Refers to a Republican secret society, founded in 1858 in America, which came to epitomize the physical force movement.

HARRY FERGUSON
His name lives on in the name of the Massey Ferguson company.

Ferguson, Harry *(1884–1960)* Engineer and mechanic from Co. Down who invented the first low-cost tractor and a way of pulling a plough whilst controlling it from the cab. He built up his company before selling to Ford and later, Massey Harris.

Ferguson, Howard *(1908–1999)* Belfast-born composer; his most famous works are the *Piano Sonata in F Minor* and *Five Bagatelles for Piano*.

Ferguson, Samuel *(1810–1886)* Poet who held trusted positions as First Deputy Keeper of Public Records of Ireland and president of the *Royal Irish Academy*.

Fermanagh, County County in the south-west of Northern Ireland. It has several areas of rural tourist interest, such as *Lough Erne* and *Enniskillen Castle*.

Fianna A legendary group of Irish warriors whose adventures are often recounted in Irish stories and folk ballads.

FIANNA FÁIL
Éamon de Valera celebrates winning the elections in 1932.

Fianna Fáil Political party in the Republic of Ireland founded by *Éamon de Valera* in 1926. Its current leader is Micheál Martin.

Fianna Fáil came into being following a split within *Sinn Féin* when they refused to enter parliament after the *Anglo-Irish Treaty*. It soon became the largest political party due to its appeal to all aspects of society. Seven of its eight leaders have served as *Taoiseach* and it was still the largest party sitting in parliament until 2011. However, following the country's economic problems it lost a lot of support in that year's election.

ENDA KENNY
Addressing the crowd after
winning the 2011 elections
and becoming Taoiseach.

Film Company of Ireland Prominent film company during the silent movie period. It made 20 films between 1916 and 1920.

Film Institute, Irish (IFI) An organisation housing the Irish Film Archive. It also promotes media studies and runs an art house cinema.

Fine Gael Political party founded in 1933; it is usually the main opposition party to *Fianna Fáil*. It was associated with the middle classes and anyone who agreed with the *Anglo-Irish Treaty*. Its current leader is Enda Kenny. It has gained power in the form of various coalitions with the Labour Party and, on occasion, with small liberal parties also. Fine Gael gained 76 seats in the 2011 election, following a lack of public confidence in Fianna Fáil. Enda Kenny went on to broker a deal with the Labour party, forming a coalition government. This was Fine Gael's first time in power since 1997 and Kenny went on to become *Taoiseach*.

Finn mac Cumhaill A mythical Irish hero and warrior.

Fishing Ireland is a top destination for fishing and is popular for angling holidays. Irish waters boast a mixture of game and coarse fishing. Irish salmon angling is internationally regarded, and there is an abundance of freshwater coarse fishing available where species such as pike, bream, rudd and eel may be caught. There are many fisheries and established locations, as well as unspoiled public waterways throughout the country. There is also plenty of marine life, with cod and bass all available around the Atlantic coast.

FISHING
Ireland is a popular angling destination.

Fitt, Gerry *(1926–2005)* Politician in Northern Ireland who founded the Social Democratic and Labour Party (SDLP). However, he resigned in 1979 and chose to sit as an independent. His home in Belfast was firebombed in 1983, one month after he was given a British peerage as Lord Fitt.

FitzGerald Anglo-Irish dynasty founded by the Anglo-Norman invader, Maurice FitzGerald, in the 12th century.

FitzGerald, Garret *(1926–2011)* Politician and leader of *Fine Gael* from 1977–87. He was instrumental in the signing of the *Anglo-Irish Agreement* of 1985. He was twice *Taoiseach* of Ireland, first from 1981–82, and again from December 1982–87. Following his death in May 2011, he was praised by international politicians, including Barack Obama, David Cameron, Enda Kenny and the then Irish president, *Mary McAleese*.

FitzGerald, George Francis *(1851–1901)* Physicist whose theories were reinterpreted by Einstein in his theory of relativity. His other theories suggested ways to transmit radio waves, as well as helping to explain the motion of the earth.

GARRET FITZGERALD
And Margaret Thatcher signed the Anglo-Irish Agreement in 1985.

F

Flag First presented in 1848 as a nationalist symbol, it is now used in the Republic of Ireland as the civil and state national flag, as well as the naval ensign. The green represents Irish natives (Catholics), the orange represents the descendants of British settlers (Protestants) and the white in between symbolises a hope for truce between the two.

THE IRISH FLAG
Because of its constitutional status, there is often debate over the usage of this flag in Northern Ireland.

Flatley, Michael *(1958–)* Irish-American dancer who revived traditional Irish dancing and brought it to an international audience with the show *Riverdance*. In 2011, Michael was introduced into the Irish American Hall of Fame.

Florence Court 18th-century house in *County Fermanagh*. It is owned by the National Trust.

ST JOHN'S WORT
Often used as a remedy for depression.

MAIDENHAIR FERN
It can shed water without getting wet.

Flowers of Ireland (Flora)
Ireland has quite a small flora
for a European country. Most
of Ireland's habitats can be
divided into grassland, heath and
bog, each of which has its own
specific flora. Other specialized
plant communities are found in
botanical sites such as sand dunes,
salt marshes, mountains, or
Ireland's most famous botanical
site, the *Burren* in Co. Clare,
which combines alpine and
Mediterranean species.

Folklore Folklore has survived in Ireland from early times to the present day. The phenomenon has proved a popular way of valuing Irish cultural difference.

Irish *literature* emerged in the 6th century, with storytellers quickly latching on to the popularity of hero-tales of ancient warriors, as well as tales of wisdom, fairies, legends, ghost stories and accounts of famous saints, such as *Saint Patrick*.

HERO-TALES
Are the basis of much of Irish folklore.

Folklore was originally passed orally through the generations. However, in 1926 The Folklore of Ireland Society was founded and has since collected a large amount of data – it even functions as a department at University College Dublin.

F

Food and Drink The most celebrated food in Ireland is the potato. There are many traditional dishes made from potato, the most famous being the farl (or fadge), which is a triangular piece of potato cake more common in the northern counties. Colcannon, also a popular dish, is mashed potatoes with spring onions and kale, or cabbage. Boxty is a unique kind of bread made with raw, grated potato. Bacon is a staple food and is a key ingredient in coddle. Black pudding (a sausage made from pig's blood) is also popular. Mutton and lamb are often used for pies and stews. Salmon, mackerel, trout and eel are popular fish; native oysters were once very common, but are now concentrated on the west coast and there is an oyster festival in *Galway* every year.

IRISH STEW
A popular dish served in many Irish pubs.

Ireland has a strong bread tradition with many varieties, from the famous soda bread to barm brack – a spicy and slightly sweet fruit bread that is popular at Hallowe'en, as legend has it that various objects baked into the bread predict the future.

Ireland's most famous drinks are *Guinness* and *whiskey*. Irish stout, such as Guinness, is made from roasting malt or barley; it gained a reputation for being a healthy, strengthening drink. Whiskey is made from distilling fermented grains; most Irish whiskeys are distilled three times before consumption. Other Irish drinks include red lemonade, which is a popular mixer for spirits, and Irish Breakfast Tea, which was produced as a blend for the USA, but in Ireland it is simply called 'tea', and is usually served strong.

SODA BREAD
There are many varieties of soda bread, some with regional characteristics.

F

Football Association of Ireland (**FAI**) Set up in 1921, its first international game was against Italy in 1926. Ireland have qualified for the World Cup Finals three times (1990, 1994 and 2002).

Football, Gaelic Kicking and catching game native to Ireland; its goalposts are similar to those of *hurling* and *camogie* with similar scoring and rules. It was first played in 1712 and is now under the

GAELIC FOOTBALL
Is one of Ireland's most popular sports.

umbrella of the *Gaelic Athletic Association (GAA)*. The All-Ireland Championship final is played in September every year.

Fricker, Brenda *(1944–)* Actress who had a long theatre and TV career before winning an Academy Award in 1990 for her performance as Christy Brown's mother in *My Left Foot*.

Friel, Brian *(1929–2015)* Dramatist and author; he is often referred to as the 'Irish Chekhov'. His work often reflects social and political issues in Irish society. His plays were written through the 1960s to the 1990s and reflect the evolution of Irish society.

BRENDA FRICKER
Winning her Academy Award in 1990.

Gaelic Athletic Association (**GAA**) An amateur Irish cultural and
sporting organisation focused primarily on promoting Gaelic games.

GAA FOOTBALL CHAMPIONSHIP WINNERS 21ST CENTURY

Year	Venue	Attendance	Winner	Score	Runner-up	Score
2000	Croke Park	64,094	Kerry	0-17	Galway	1-10
2001	Croke Park	70,842	Galway	0-17	Meath	0-8
2002	Croke Park	79,500	Armagh	1-12	Kerry	0-14
2003	Croke Park	79,394	Tyrone	0-12	Armagh	0-9
2004	Croke Park	79,749	Kerry	1-20	Mayo	2-9
2005	Croke Park	82,112	Tyrone	1-16	Kerry	2-10
2006	Croke Park	82,289	Kerry	4-15	Mayo	3-5
2007	Croke Park	82,126	Kerry	3-13	Cork	1-9
2008	Croke Park	82,204	Tyrone	1-15	Kerry	0-14
2009	Croke Park	82,246	Kerry	0-16	Cork	1-9
2010	Croke Park	81,604	Cork	0-16	Down	0-15
2011	Croke Park	82,300	Dublin	1-12	Kerry	1-11
2012	Croke Park	82,274	Kilkenny	3-22	Galway	3-11
2013	Croke Park	82,756	Clare	5-16	Cork	3-16
2014	Croke Park	82,184	Kerry	2-9	Donegal	0-12
2015	Croke Park	82,243	Dublin	0-12	Kerry	0-9

Gaeltacht The word used to refer to areas of Ireland where Irish is spoken. These areas are mostly in the south and west of the Republic of Ireland. Gaeltachts are seen as the preservers of Irish heritage and often receive grants to help maintain enthusiasm for Irish radio, TV and playhouses.

IRISH SIGNS
Are very common in Gaeltacht areas, and some do not have English translations.

Gallagher, Rory *(1948–1995)* Singer, songwriter, and multi-instrumentalist who was one of the first Irish musicians to embrace rock and roll. He was part of the band Taste and toured throughout the world.

COUNTY GALWAY
Has a dense population
of flora and fauna.

GALWAY BAY
A popular tourist destination,
even in winter.

Galtee Mountains Mountain range stretching between *County Tipperary* and *County Limerick*. The rock is made of red sandstone and quartzite. The valley between the mountains has been the scene of many ancient battles.

Galway, County Situated on the west coast of the Republic of Ireland. It has many features, including the *Aran Islands*, *Lough Derg*, dramatic mountain ranges, cathedrals, castles and forts. It is the second-largest county in Ireland and its main industries are tourism and textiles.

Galway, City A coastal city popular for salmon and eel fishing. It is home to the *National University of Ireland* and the *Taibhdhearc* theatre. The city was founded in the 12th century and parts of the town's original walls can still be seen today. It is the third-largest city in the Republic of Ireland. The Irish name for Galway is *Gaillimh*, meaning 'stony river'.

Galway, James *(1939–)* Virtuoso flute player, who played with top orchestras around the world before beginning a career as a soloist. He was awarded an OBE in 1977 and knighted in 2001.

Garda Síochána Police force in the Republic of Ireland established in 1922, around the time of the *Anglo-Irish Treaty* and the Irish *Civil War*. It functions, for the most part, unarmed. Since the 1970s and the *Troubles*, the force has expanded greatly, with divisions specialising in terrorism and national security.

Gately, Stephen *(1976–2009)* Member of the boyband *Boyzone*, he shared lead vocals with fellow band member, *Ronan Keating*. He also appeared in various stage shows and had a brief career as a solo artist.

He died suddenly in Majorca in 2009 from an undiagnosed heart condition. An article in the UK *Daily Mail* that linked his death to a 'homosexual lifestyle' received over 25,000 complaints in one day.

STEPHEN GATELY
Shared the majority of lead vocals in Boyzone.

Gate Theatre Founded in Dublin in 1928, it has a reputation for modernist works, international plays and experimental theatre.

Geldof, Bob *(1954–)* The lead singer of the Boomtown Rats. He is most famous for setting up the charity Band Aid with Midge Ure and other pop celebrities in the 1980s. He raised £60 million for famine relief in Africa with the Band Aid song, *Do They Know It's Christmas?* In 1985 he staged two Live Aid concerts to raise more money. He was knighted in 1986 and was also nominated for a Nobel Peace Prize.

LIVE AID
Had an estimated global audience of 1.9 billion.

G

Geography Ireland is an island; it is situated on the north-western edge of Europe. It is often called the Emerald Isle due to its green landscapes. Its geographical features are made up of low-lying plains and rugged coastlines. There are many lakes and rivers – the longest river is the *River Shannon* and the largest lake is *Lough Neagh*. It lies 8 degrees west of England and is separated from the British mainland by the *Irish Sea*. The rest of Europe lies to the south and is separated by the Celtic Sea. To the west of Ireland is the Atlantic Ocean, which separates it from America. Ireland has a temperate climate, despite its geographical location – this is due to the warm seas of the North Atlantic Drift (Gulf Stream).

THE IRISH LANDSCAPE
The banks of the River Shannon.

G

Giant's Causeway, The One of Ireland's most popular tourist attractions, it lies on the north coast of *County Antrim*. It is a formation of basalt columns caused by solidified lava from the tertiary period. Irish *folklore* claims the causeway was built by the folk hero *Finn mac Cumhaill* so that giants could cross the gap between Ireland and Scotland. It became a World Heritage Site in 1986.

THE GIANT'S CAUSEWAY
The distinctive basalt columns are a popular tourist attraction.

Glendalough Monastic site and mountainous area containing medieval remains of a Christian settlement. It is also a popular destination for rock climbing and rambling.

GLENDALOUGH
The upper lake.

Gogarty, Oliver St John *(1878–1957)* Writer, surgeon and politician. He was senator of the Irish Free State from 1922–36. He was close friends with *W. B. Yeats* and other literary figures. Although his autobiographical novel, *As I Was Going Down Sackville Street*, was the subject of a libel case, he is best remembered for his racier books, *Tumbling In The Hay* and *It Isn't This Time Of Year At All!*

Goldsmith, Oliver *(1728–1774)* Playwright and author whose narratives strongly favoured rural life over urban society.

Golf Golf has been an established sport in Ireland since the 1800s. The Golfing Union of Ireland, established in 1891, is the oldest in the world. Ireland has staged many high-profile golf tournaments and has produced many top golfers.

Gonne, Maud *(1866–1953)* Born in Surrey the daughter of an army officer, she was educated in Ireland and London and by the age of 20 was a confirmed Irish nationalist. Independently wealthy, she devoted herself to the cause of Irish independence. Her charisma and beauty won her numerous admirers, most notably *W. B. Yeats*. She had two children (one deceased) with her French lover, Lucien Millevoye, and one son, Seán MacBride, with her husband, Major John MacBride, whom she later divorced. She refused numerous offers of marriage from Yeats, but they remained friends for life.

MAUD GONNE
Turned down a number of marriage proposals from W. B. Yeats.

Good Friday Agreement, The *(1998)* The name given to the 1998 Belfast Agreement between the United Kingdom and the Republic of Ireland. It was a major step forward on the road to peace in Northern Ireland. Following *Bloody Sunday* and many more acts of violence during the *Troubles*, Britain was desperate to find a way to end the violence.

PEACE STATUE, DERRY
Symbolises the peace for which the community is striving.

Over 20 years of tense peace talks resulted in the Belfast Agreement. It stated that Northern Ireland would keep the same status and would only change with a majority vote from its citizens. At the same time the Republic of Ireland relinquished its territorial claim over Northern Ireland. Most important was the promise from both sides that they would use only peaceful methods in future negotiations.

G

HENRY GRATTAN
A cartoon from an
Irish newspaper.

GRAND CANAL
In County Laois.

Grand Canal Two rival schemes
were presented to the Irish Parliament in
1756 to link Dublin to the River Shannon.
After many delays, the canal was opened in
1805. It flows through the counties of
Kildare, *Offaly*, *Dublin* and *Laois*.

Grattan, Henry *(1746–1820)* Nationalist
politician who campaigned for free trade and
Irish independence in the 1780s. He retired
from politics after becoming disillusioned
with Protestantism in parliament.

Graves, Alfred Perceval *(1846–1931)*
Poet who played a key role in the Irish
literary revival. He also worked for the Home
Office and became an inspector for schools.

Graves, Robert James *(1796–1853)* Doctor
who specialised in diagnosis. His name is
used for the condition Graves' Disease,
which is an enlargement of the thyroid gland.
He introduced radical reforms into the Irish
health service, most notably regarding the
treatment of patients with a fever.

Grave slabs Flat stones that are usually
decorated with crosses and Celtic designs,
dating from the early Christian period.
More than 800 are known.

ALFRED PERCEVAL GRAVES
He was a key figure in
the Irish literary revival
of the 1930s.

GRAVE SLABS
From the late medieval
period in Kildalton church.

ARTHUR GRIFFITH
Founder of the political
party Sinn Féin.

HOWARD GRUBB
Invented the first
usable periscope.

Griffth, Arthur *(1872–1922)* Politician; he founded the political party Sinn Féin and became the first president of Dáil Éireann in 1922. Although he was a printer by trade, he became involved in Nationalist politics. He joined the *Irish Volunteers* and participated in their secret arms deals; however, he played no part in the *Easter Rising*. His goal was for an Irish dual-monarchy and economic independence.
He died of a cerebral haemorrhage only seven months after becoming president.

Grubb, Howard *(1844–1931)* An engineer who is famous for developing the first useful submarine periscope.

Guerin, Veronica *(1958–1996)* Crime reporter who managed to uncover drug lords and money launderers despite threats and intimidation against her. She made many remarkable discoveries, which led to her murder in 1996.

GUINNESS
Guinness is now owned by the multinational company Diageo.

Guildford Four Four Irishmen who were wrongly convicted of terrorist attacks in Guildford in 1974. They were released 14 years later when it transpired that Surrey police had given ambiguous evidence at trial.

Guinness Ireland's best-known beer, generally considered the national drink of Ireland. The Guinness company is the world's largest brewer of stout. It was established in 1759 and by the early 20th century, it was the seventh-largest company in the world. Its adverts have won many awards and its most memorable slogan, 'Guinness is good for you', first appeared in 1929. Its Dublin brewery produces 810 million pints per year.

Gur, Lough Lake situated in *County Limerick*. It is famous for being the site of many Neolithic Age ruins, including tombs, graves and ring forts. Archaeologists have found pieces dating back to the Stone Age, as well as bones of now extinct native animals.

H

Hamilton, William Rowan *(1805–1865)* Well-respected astronomer and mathematician who worked in optics and dynamics; he also contributed to our understanding of algebra.

Harp The harp is the national instrument of Ireland. Harping was a skill that defined Irish aristocracy and the tradition was passed through generations. The harping tradition began to go out of fashion in the 16th century and by the 19th century it was almost obsolete. The traditional Irish harp, unlike its modern-day equivalent, was non-chromatic and is referred to by musicologists as a 'neo-Irish' harp. Ireland's most famous harpist is *Turlough Carolan*.

HARP
The national instrument of Ireland.

Harrington, Pádraig *(1971–)* Professional golfer who won major championships in 2007 and 2008. He currently plays on the European and PGA Tours.

Harris, Richard *(1930–2002)* Actor who is best known for his role as Dumbledore in the first two films of the Harry Potter franchise. He starred in many other films; when asked about his role in Harry Potter, he said he hoped it would not be the only thing he was remembered for. He also hit the UK charts in 1968 with the song 'MacArthur Park'.

Haughey, Charles James *(1925–2006)* The fourth leader of *Fianna Fáil*, he served three terms as *Taoiseach*, from 1979–81, in 1982, and from 1987–92. A staunch Republican, he was in office during the difficult period of the *hunger strikes*. One of the dominant political figures of his generation, his career was marked by a series of scandals, and his reputation suffered as a result of findings of corruption against him.

PÁDRAIG HARRINGTON

He has won three major championships in his career.

Healthcare The healthcare system in the Republic of Ireland evolved from the workhouse system. A dispensary system divided the country into manageable areas. The dispensary system made healthcare available to rural areas and soon hospitals appeared. In 1947 an emphasis was placed on treating epidemics such as tuberculosis, as well as education on preventable diseases. Since then the health system has expanded to deal with 'modern' diseases such as drug abuse and mental illness and is administered by the Health Service Executive (HSE). Fees for medical services are payable by all except those on low incomes and many Irish residents pay for private health insurance.

GENERAL HOSPITAL
In South Tipperary.

Heaney, Seamus *(1939–2013)* Poet from *County Derry*. His critically acclaimed poetry is powerful and hard-hitting; it depicts rural life in Ireland and often reflected the political situation in Northern Ireland at the time. His most famous works include *The Spirit Level*, *Opened Ground: Poems 1966–1996* and *The Redress of Poetry*. He received many awards, the most notable being the Nobel Prize for Literature in 1995 and the T. S. Eliot prize in 2006. His work is highly regarded throughout the world and has played an important role in the evolution of contemporary poetry.

SEAMUS HEANEY
His work is studied extensively in all Irish schools, as well as in UK schools, and is the basis of many exam syllabuses.

Heaney has had university buildings named after him and has inspired many generations. He had surprising praise for rapper Eminem, who, he thought, could 'inspire a generation'.

HENRY VIII
The catalyst of the Catholic/Protestant divide in both the UK and Ireland.

Henry VIII *(1491–1547)*
King of England who is best known for his six wives. His biggest impact on Ireland came with the creation of the Church of England and the dissolution of the monasteries. He rejected Catholicism for mainly political reasons, due to Italian influence on the Pope, but also because he wished to divorce his wife. At this time, English control stretched only as far as *The English Pale*. Although the Catholic majority were slow to conform to the new methods of land ownership following the dissolution of the monasteries, as more and more Protestant settlers from England came to Ireland and laid claim to Irish land, the Catholic/Protestant divide took root.

Hedge Schools Secret schools that existed during the 17th, 18th and 19th centuries when Catholic schools were outlawed, a move that was aimed at trying to force the Catholic middle classes to convert to the Church of England, so that their children would receive a good education. Hedge schools got their name because they were taught outdoors to avoid discovery. The lessons were usually given orally from educated men in the community.

Higgins, Alex *(1949–2010)* Snooker player who was nicknamed 'Hurricane Higgins' because of how fast he played the game. He was the youngest player to win the Embassy World Championship in 1972.

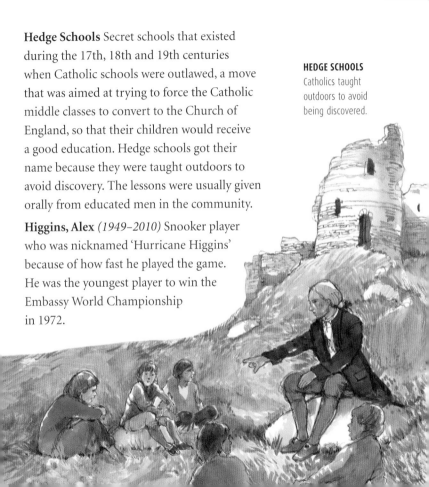

HEDGE SCHOOLS
Catholics taught outdoors to avoid being discovered.

History Evidence of human settlement in Ireland dates back to between 8000 and 6000 BC (the Mesolithic Age). Few traces of these civilisations remain, but some can still be seen around the island.

Later the *Celts* arrived and introduced their language, art and culture. Christianity was introduced to the country in AD 432 by *Saint Patrick* and only a few hundred years later, *Viking* invasions brought chaos to the monastic institutions and religious ways of life. However, the Irish were strong enough to survive.

MICHAEL COLLINS

Was an influential figure in Irish history. He campaigned for Irish independence, which led to the Anglo-Irish Treaty. Some believed it was not enough. He was assassinated in 1922, by those who opposed the treaty, during the Irish Civil War.

The coming of the Normans in the 12th century began the start of English involvement in Ireland. The 16th and 17th centuries was the period of *plantation,* which saw the influx of many English settlers in Ireland. Catholics lost much of their land, as well as political influence, during this time. A Protestant minority influenced key political moves during the 18th century. The 19th century saw rebellion from Catholic groups and the Irish made moves to separate from British rule. *The Easter Rising* of 1916 forced a Republican agenda to the forefront once again and eventually led to the division of Ireland into Northern Ireland and the Irish Free State (now the Republic of Ireland) in 1920. The Irish State made a moral claim over Northern Ireland, which lasted officially until the 1998 *Good Friday Agreement*. Modern history has been dominated by the conflict between Nationalists and Unionists in Northern Ireland, which came to a head in the late 1960s during the *Troubles*.

Hockey Hockey is a leading sport in Ireland, particularly women's hockey. It was introduced in the 19th century and since then Ireland has taken part in many top international competitions, including the Olympic Games.

Holidays Ireland is a popular place for holidaymakers. It boasts miles and miles of unspoiled coastline, as well as many places of historical interest, with ruins dating back to the dawn of civilisation. Its lakes and rivers are popular for angling holidays, due to an abundance of fish and clean, unspoiled waters. The countryside is popular for hiking and walking holidays, with lots of *flora* and *fauna* to be seen. The large cities of *Dublin* and *Belfast* attract city-break holidaymakers keen on experiencing Irish life, *architecture*, *food* and culture.

NORTHERN IRELAND Is a popular tourist destination; the Giant's Causeway receives thousands of visitors each year.

H

Holland, John Phillip *(1840–1914)* Engineer who developed military submarines, initially to help Irish Republican groups build an underwater vessel that could attack England.

Home Rule A Nationalist movement that aimed to extricate Ireland from British rule. Many of the Protestants in Ulster feared the movement, as they were worried about being dominated by a Catholic majority. The movement led to the *Partition* of Ireland and the establishment of the *Irish Free State*.

BRITISH PARLIAMENT
Was concerned about an Irish uprising, which is why Home Rule was always rejected by Britain.

Horse Racing Horse racing is extremely popular in Ireland. Its origin can be traced back to early competitions that took place around AD 200. Flat racing, as well as steeplechasing, gained popularity during the 19th century, with money being invested in breeding, training and racecourses. Horse racing is a lucrative industry; Ireland has 27 racecourses, the most famous being Leopardstown Park in *Dublin* and the *Curragh* in *County Kildare*.

HORSE RACING
Is one of Ireland's most lucrative industries.

JOHN HUME
Was a key figure in the Northern Ireland Peace Process.

HUMEWOOD CASTLE
Used as a location during the filming of *The Tudors*.

Huguenots French Protestants who were banished from France and emigrated to Ireland around 1690.

Hume, John *(1937–)* Politician in Northern Ireland who was leader of the *SDLP* party from 1979–2001. He received the Nobel Peace Prize in 1998 for his work to help the ongoing peace process in Northern Ireland, which culminated in the 1998 *Good Friday Agreement*.

Humewood Castle Large country house estate in *County Wicklow* used in the filming of the TV series *The Tudors*. Bought in 2013 by American billionare, John Malone.

Hunger strikes Hunger striking was a tactic used by Irish Republican prisoners from 1917 as a way of negotiating better conditions. Hunger strikes usually had little success and attracted minimal sympathy. However, in the early 1980s the deaths of ten Republicans, including popular MP Bobby Sands, resulted in the emergence of *Sinn Féin* as a real political force in Northern Ireland.

HUNGER STRIKE
Memorial in Milltown Cemetery, Belfast.

Hurling National game that dates back to the time of the Celts. *Camogie* is the women's equivalent. It is played with 15 players on each side with the aim of the game being to get the ball, called the 'sliotar', over or through the opposition's goalposts using sticks. The goalposts are H-shaped like rugby posts.

HURLING
A uniquely Irish sport.

TOP 10 PERFORMING HURLING TEAMS

	Team	Number of All-Ireland Championship Wins	Winning Years
1	Kilkenny	36	1904, 1905, 1907, 1909, 1911, 1912, 1913, 1922, 1932, 1933, 1935, 1939, 1947, 1957, 1963, 1967, 1969, 1972, 1974, 1975, 1979, 1982, 1983, 1992, 1993, 2000, 2002, 2003, 2006, 2007, 2008, 2009, 2011, 2012, 2014, 2015
2	Cork	30	1890, 1892, 1893, 1894, 1902, 1903, 1919, 1926, 1928, 1929, 1931, 1941, 1942, 1943, 1944, 1946, 1952, 1953, 1954, 1966, 1970, 1976, 1977, 1978, 1984, 1986, 1990, 1999, 2004, 2005
3	Tipperary	26	1887, 1895, 1896, 1898, 1899, 1900, 1906, 1908, 1916, 1925, 1930, 1937, 1945, 1949, 1950, 1951, 1958, 1961, 1962, 1964, 1965, 1971, 1989, 1991, 2001, 2010
4	Limerick	7	1897, 1918, 1921, 1934, 1936, 1940, 1973
5	Dublin	6	1889, 1917, 1920, 1924, 1927, 1938
6	Wexford	6	1910, 1955, 1956, 1960, 1968, 1996
7	Galway	4	1923, 1980, 1987, 1988
8	Offaly	4	1981, 1985, 1994, 1998
9	Clare	4	1914, 1995, 1997, 2013
10	Waterford	2	1948, 1959

WALTER OSBORNE
In A Dublin Park: Light and Shade from 1895.

Impressionists Group of Irish artists who studied and worked abroad in France, Belgium, London and Rome during the late 19th and early 20th centuries. The reason for many artists moving to these areas could have been due to the greater diversity and training available in these places and also because, at this time, aristocratic patronage had largely died out.

The main members were *Nathaniel Hone*, Frank O'Meara, *John Lavery*, Sarah Purser, *Edith Somerville* and *Walter Osborne*. Unlike other Irish emigrants at that time, they had no political agenda and their work focused on portraits, landscapes and naturalism.

CATTLE FARMING
Ireland's land
lends itself to the
agricultural industry.

SALMON
Many of Ireland's maritime bays
are used for salmon farming.

Industry The main industries that drive the Irish economy today are mining, food production, *agriculture*, pharmaceuticals, machinery, railway transport, glass, digital media, software development and *tourism*.

Exports of raw materials play an important role in Ireland's economy. Ireland is the seventh-largest producer of zinc in the world and the largest in Europe.

Ireland's main economic resource, however, is its expanse of fertile lands and clean waterways. Cattle, beef and dairy products and fish account for a large percentage of Ireland's exports, although the fishing industry has suffered from overfishing since 1995.

The recent economic downturn, coupled with less demand for new residential housing, has meant that the construction industry has declined since 2008, from a share of almost 20 per cent of economic activity to just under 5 per cent.

ILLUMINATED MANUSCRIPTS
Are the best examples of
Insular Art.

INLA MURAL
In Bogside, Derry.

"YEARS FROM NOW THEY WILL ASK YOU WHERE YOU WERE WHEN YOUR COMRADES WERE DYING ON HUNGERSTRIKE, SHALL YOU SAY YOU WERE WITH US OR SHALL YOU SAY THAT YOU WERE CONFORMING TO THE VERY SYSTEM THAT DROVE US TO OUR DEATHS"

INLA (The Irish National Liberation Army)
A rogue organisation that has its origins in the *IRA*. Initially the INLA rejected the peace process, but after the *Omagh Bombing*, it became the first organisation of its type to support moves towards peace.

Insular Art A style of art originating from Celtic Christianity. The best examples of this are in illuminated manuscripts, such as the *Book of Kells*.

Internment The term used for the detention of prisoners without trial, usually for those suspected of terrorist attacks. Notable uses of this were after the *Easter Rising* in 1916, during the *War of Independence* and *IRA* bombing campaigns.

Invincibles, the A group of Irish terrorists who set out to make a series of key assassinations, however, their only real success came with the *Phoenix Park Murders* of 1882.

IRA MURALS
Were painted on the sides of many houses.

IRA BRIGADE
Taken during the War of Independence.

IRA The Irish Republican Army, founded in 1919 by Michael Collins as the military wing of the political party *Sinn Féin*. Its aim was for a united Ireland under Irish rule. The IRA's initial goal was to combat British rule by force. In 1922 the IRA split over the Treaty, dividing into pro- and anti-Treaty factions, which led to the *Civil War*. The IRA became a secret organization and was declared illegal in 1936. The violence escalated during the late 1960s, a period referred to as the *Troubles*. In 1969 the IRA split, with the *Provisional IRA* continuing terrorist activities in Britain and Northern Ireland. There were ceasefires during the 1990s and splinter groups emerged – the extremist *Real IRA* carried out the infamous car bomb attack in Omagh in 1998.

Ireland, Republic of The south of Ireland. It is made up of 26 counties and its capital is *Dublin*. It was originally known as the *Irish Free State*.

Irish Citizen Army A small group of volunteers made up of union workers. It was put together initially as a defence force for workers during demonstrations. It took part in the *Easter Rising* under *James Connolly*.

IRISH DANCING
Traditional Irish dance has been passed down through the generations.

Irish Dancing The two main types of traditional Irish dancing are step dancing and céili dancing. Step dancing is often performed as a solo and involves stylised, rhythmic movement of the feet without moving the upper body. This style of dancing was made famous in 1994 by the international phenomenon, *Riverdance*. Céili dancing is a traditional folk dance involving lines of dancers facing each other, often in pairs, who then progress in a set pattern. Céili dancing is often performed at a céilidh, which is an Irish social gathering.

Irish Film Board Set up by the government to promote indigenous productions, it is funded by the Arts Council. Board members in the past included *Gabriel Byrne* and *Neil Jordan*.

Irish Free State Established in 1922 following the *Anglo-Irish Treaty*. In 1937, the Irish Free State became *Éire* and later, in 1949, the Republic of Ireland.

Irish Independence Ireland had been independent until the Norman invasion, which marked the start of British rule in Ireland. After many rebellions and bloody battles, Ireland became independent once more in 1921 following *partition* and the *Anglo-Irish Treaty*, which created the *Irish Free State*. *Northern Ireland*, however, remained part of the UK.

IRISH REBELLIONS
Happened throughout the ages, the most famous being the Rebellion of 1798.

Irish Land Acts Laws passed in the late 1800s that were designed to improve life for Irish peasants. The laws meant tenants were paid for work done on their land and were protected against rent increases. It also put in place systems to help tenants buy land from their landlords.

IRISH MUSEUM OF MODERN ART
Was established in 1990.

IMMA (Irish Museum of Modern Art) Established in 1990, the museum opened in 1991 in the 17th-century Royal Hospital Kilmainham in Dublin. The museum houses Ireland's largest collection of modern and contemporary art and presents it in a wide variety of programmes and exhibitions. Entrance to the museum is free.

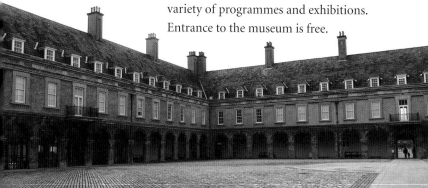

Irish Press The popularity of Irish newspapers is directly related to the rise in literacy during the 18th century and the reduced tax status of newspapers in the early 1800s. The first ever English-language newspaper was *The News Letter*, which was founded and published in *Belfast* in 1737. In Southern Ireland, *The Nation*, first published in 1842, had a strong Nationalist following. Provincial papers became hugely popular, with more than 60 papers serving local news to their communities during the 1800s. Irish newspapers were often very politicised, although, in recent times they have placed more emphasis on social events, sports and entertainment. The main newspapers in Northern Ireland are *The Irish News* and *The Belfast News Letter*. The main newspapers in the Republic of Ireland are *The Irish Times* and *The Irish Independent*. There are a number of newspapers printed in Irish, including *Foinse*.

THE NATION
A Nationalist newspaper first printed in 1842. It often published influential political articles.

THE FENIAN EXECUTIVE
The founding members of the Irish Republican Brotherhood.

Irish Republican Brotherhood Secret society related to the *Fenian* movement. Membership favoured *Irish independence* and was influential in the *Easter Rising*. The organization disbanded following the *Anglo-Irish Treaty*, although rumours that it still exists in the USA are rife.

Irish Sea The body of water that forms part of the Atlantic Ocean; it separates Ireland from England and Wales.

Irish Volunteers Military group set up to force the issue of *Home Rule* in 1913. *Robert Erskine Childers* helped the volunteers smuggle guns and ammunition into the country. The Irish Volunteers became infiltrated by the *Irish Republican Brotherhood* and later became involved in the *Easter Rising*, as a result of which many of its members were executed.

IWWU (Irish Women Workers' Union) A women-only workers' union; its aim was to improve worker-employer relations. They campaigned against parts of the 1937 *Constitution*, which compromised working opportunities for women. The IWWU merged with the Federated Workers' Union of Ireland in 1984.

Irish Yeomanry A reserve military force set up to help defend against attacks from the *United Irishmen* during the *Rebellion of 1798*. The majority of the yeomen were Protestant. It was disbanded in 1834.

Irvine, Eddie *(1965–)* Formula 1 racing driver from *County Down*. His professional career began in 1983 when he raced in the Formula Ford Championships. He was picked up in 1993 by *Eddie Jordan*'s Ferrari team, where he partnered Michael Schumacher.

EDDIE IRVINE
At the USA Grand Prix in 2002.

JEDWARD
Performing on the
ITV show, *The X Factor*.

Jennings, Pat *(1945–)* Professional footballer from *County Down*. He played goalkeeper, most notably for the English teams Tottenham Hotspur and Arsenal. He also played for the Northern Ireland national team in 119 matches.

Jedward *(1991–)* Novelty pop act featuring identical twins John and Edward Grimes. They found fame on *The X Factor* and are now managed by their mentor from the show, *Louis Walsh*. Their first single reached number two in the UK charts and number one in the Irish charts.

John F. Kennedy Arboretum

A memorial in *County Wexford* dedicated to the memory of the former US president, who served from 1961 until his assassination in 1963. It is situated there because it overlooks the ancestral home of the Kennedys.

The arboretum is a plant collection spanning 252 hectares (623 acres) and it contains over 4,500 different types of trees, as well as plants, shrubs and hedges. It also features a waterfall. Guided tours are available between April and September every year.

Joly, John *(1857–1933)* Geologist who was one of the first to use radioactive methods as a way of determining the age of rocks. He also spearheaded the treatment of cancer through radiotherapy.

JOHN F. KENNEDY
Just one of his many memorials around the world, the arboretum is situated in County Wexford.

Jordan, Eddie *(1948–)* Formula 1 team owner who started in Formula 3 before entering a team in Formula 1 in 1991. He won his first grand prix in 1998 with a first and second place finish from his two drivers, Damon Hill and Ralf Schumacher. The team was initially sold to Midland Group in 2005 and has been sold several times since; it is now owned by Force India. Eddie Jordan is now a BBC sports analyst for motor racing.

Jordan, Neil *(1950–)* Film director and writer, he is best known for the Academy Award-winning *The Crying Game* (1992) and *Interview With the Vampire: The Vampire Chronicles* (1994).

Joyce, James *(1882–1941)* Novelist best known for his books *Ulysses* (1922) and *Finnegans Wake* (1939), both of which are regarded as works of art, as well as difficult to read and understand, due to the many linguistic experiments used.

JAMES JOYCE
One of the most influential writers of the 20th century.

Judiciary Irish justice is administered by the Supreme Court, the High Court, the Circuit Court and the District Court. Each court has its own judges and presidents; the Chief Justice is the head of the judiciary. In the past, appointments to the judiciary have been considered politically motivated. The Judicial Appointments Advisory Board was set up as a result of this controversy in 1995.

In Northern Ireland, judges are appointed according to the British system, which is through the monarch or the prime minister. Northern Ireland has its own Lord Chief Justice, who is President of the Court of Appeal, the High Court and the Crown Court.

THE FOUR COURTS, DUBLIN
The main court buildings in Ireland.

This memorial is on the north side of the Grand Canal in Dublin.

Kavanagh, Patrick *(1904–1967)* Poet from *County Monaghan*. His unromantic view of the Irish peasantry led to critical acclaim and he is now recognised as one of Ireland's greatest poets, whose views on poverty and religion resonated with many readers.

Keane, John B. *(1928–2002)* Playwright whose work reflected the changing times in Ireland during the 1950s and 1960s.

Keane, Robbie *(1980–)* Footballer who has played in the UK and the USA. He was the youngest player to score for the Republic of Ireland and is now the team's captain.

Keating, Ronan *(1977–)* Singer who initially found fame with boy band *Boyzone* – he shared lead vocals with *Stephen Gately* before going solo in 1999. He is well known for being a judge on the *Australian X Factor*. He publicly fell out with his manager *Louis Walsh* in 2000. He swam the Irish Sea in August 2011 to raise money for cancer research.

RONAN KEATING
Boyzone's lead vocalist.

Keating, Seán *(1889–1977)* Prolific artist whose paintings charted the development of Ireland. He painted many landscapes from the *Aran Islands* and also the development of the Shannon hydroelectric scheme.

THE BOOK OF KELLS
The most famous
illuminated manuscript.

Kells, Book of The most famous illuminated manuscript. Its origin is still a matter of controversy, with many claiming it was actually completed in Iona, Scotland. It dates back to around AD 800 and contains the four Gospels. The decoration is a classic example of *insular art* – it features Christ with the Virgin Mary, Christ's Temptation and Christ's Arrest.

Kelly, Seán *(1956–)* Professional road cyclist who has competed in many international races including the Tour de France, where he won the maillot vert (green jersey for sprinting) in 1982, and the Vuelta a España, where he was the overall winner in 1988.

Kelvin, 1st Baron, William Thomson *(1824–1907)* Engineer and inventor of the electric telegraph who was knighted by Queen Victoria for his work on the transatlantic telegraph. He is well known for his work on improving the mariner's compass. He is best known for his discovery of absolute zero and, as such, absolute temperatures are measured in units of Kelvin.

Kennelly, Brendan *(1936–)* Poet best known for avoiding the intellectual pretensions of his day, which is best displayed in his 1995 epic poem, *Poetry My Arse*. His 1991 poem, *The Book of Judas,* caused controversy when it questioned the black-and-white nature of religion.

SEÁN KELLY
Now works as a commentator.

MARINER'S COMPASS
Was greatly improved by William Thomson Kelvin.

Kerry, County Situated in the south-west of the Republic of Ireland, it features many picturesque lakes as well as ancient forts and towers. One of its greatest industries is tourism, with over one million visitors choosing to come to the area each year.

Kerry, Ring of A tourist trail in *County Kerry* featuring local attractions, such as Ross Castle, Lough Leane and Killarney National Park.

Kildare, County Situated to the east of the Irish midlands, it boasts rich pastures and is home to the *Curragh*.

Kildare, town Town in *County Kildare*. It is a popular place for commuters, being only 30 miles (50 km) from Dublin with fast train, bus and road links. It is also home to the Cathedral of *St Brigid*.

THE RING OF KERRY
A popular tourist trail.

JAPANESE GARDENS
In County Kildare.

KILKENNY CASTLE
A popular tourist attraction
in the county.

KILKENNY
An aerial view over the city.

Kilkenny, County Situated in the south of the Republic of Ireland. Its main industries are agriculture and quarrying; it is the source of the famous 'black Kilkenny marble', which is polished limestone. It became the base of wealthy Anglo-Norman settlers and the riches of this era can be seen in some of the county's architecture.

Kilkenny, City Town in County Kerry famous for its lakeside location. It is a popular tourist destination and has a rich heritage dating back to the 6th century.

KDW (Kilkenny Design Workshops) Part of a design initiative by the Irish government in the 1960s, which was inspired by similar projects in Scandinavia. It became a government-funded company until the late 20th century.

LOUGH LEANE
A beautiful part of Killarney.

Killarney, town Town in *County Kerry*. It is one of Ireland's most popular tourist destinations due to its abundance of *flora* and *fauna*, as well as boasting beautiful landscapes. It is the site of many medieval ruins, including monasteries and castles.

Kinane, Michael *(1959–)* Jockey from *County Tipperary* who was champion jockey of Ireland 13 times in his 34-year career.

King, Cecil *(1921–1986)* Abstract painter from *County Wicklow*. He was mainly self-taught and his most famous exhibition was a solo project in Dublin in 1959.

Kinsella, Thomas *(1928–)* Poet, teacher and publisher, he has published over 30 collections and translated extensively from Irish, notably the famous epic, *The Táin*. He founded the Peppercannister Press in 1972. He was granted the Freedom of the City of Dublin in 2007.

PROPAGANDA
Kitchener became famous
for his recruitment posters.

KNOCKMEALDOWN
A view of the mountain range.

Kitchener, Horatio *(1850–1916)* Politician from *County Kerry*, who served with the British Army in Egyptian conflicts and the Boer War. He is best known for his recruitment campaign following the outbreak of the Great War (World War I).

Knappogue Castle 15th-century castle in *County Clare*. A typical example of a medieval tower house. It was restored during the late 20th century and is now a popular venue for tourists and weddings.

Knock Village in *County Mayo* where apparitions of the Virgin Mary were seen in 1879. Now a popular pilgrimage site with a basilica and international airport.

Knockmealdown Mountains A mountain range in *County Tipperary*. At the highest point it is 2,608 ft (795 m).

KNOCKNAREA
This is believed to be the site of Medhbh's (Queen Maeve's) grave.

Knocknarea Ancient burial site in *County Sligo*. It is the site of an unexcavated passage tomb. Legend has it that the tomb contains the remains of Medhbh, or Queen Maeve, the ancient queen of Connacht.

Kylemore Abbey 19th-century castle commissioned by Mitchell Henry. It was sold to the Benedictines early in the 20th century and was for many years a Catholic convent school. The abbey and estate are open to visitors.

Kyteler, Alice *(1280–c.1325)* 14th-century noblewoman who, after outliving four husbands, was accused of witchcraft by the bishop of Ossory. She fled to England, but her so-called conspirators were found guilty of witchcraft and Petronilla de Meath was burned at the stake instead of Alice.

L

Labour Party Founded in 1912. In its early years it prioritised industrial action and rebellion, such as the *Easter Rising*, over electoral politics. It remains a small party, but often forms coalitions.

Land League An organisation set up by peasants who used boycotting methods to gain better living conditions from their landlords. Their actions led to the *Irish Land Acts* in the late 1800s. The word 'boycott' derives from this period of time, when an English landlord's agent called Charles Boycott opposed reform and was ostracized.

THE LAND WAR
Lasted from 1879 to 1881.

Landmarks Ireland boasts so many historical, geological and architectural landmarks that it is impossible to list them all. Some of the best-known landmarks in Ireland are:

✦ *Newgrange* tombs – You could spend a whole day experiencing the prehistoric monuments and passage tombs that lie on the *River Boyne*.

✦ *The Burren* – With its unique rock formations and ancient monuments, it is a place like no other on this earth.

✦ *The Giant's Causeway* – One of Northern Ireland's most popular tourist attractions made up of basalt columns that point to Scotland.

✦ *Dublin City* – It's small enough to visit all parts over a weekend; famous landmarks include the Spire and Dublin Castle.

✦ *Ring of Kerry* – An area of outstanding natural beauty, with lakes, castles, coastal paths and mountain landscapes.

MOLLY MALONE
This statue is a well-known landmark in the streets of Dublin.

Landscape The Irish landscape is characterised by miles of rugged coastline, acres of unspoiled pasture, idyllic lakes and mountain ranges formed during the Ice Age around 20,000 years ago. The low-lying areas are perfect for agriculture. Much of these areas are well known for their *peat bogs*, which were once lakes. The land, rivers and seashores provide homes for an array of wildlife and have also provided material for poets such as *W. B. Yeats* and artists like *Susanna Drury*.

IRISH LANDSCAPE
Is characterised by acres of unspoiled pastures.

Lane, Hugh Percy *(1875–1915)* Art dealer who founded the Municipal Gallery of Modern Art in Dublin, and was also director of the *National Gallery of Ireland*. He died during World War I on the ill-fated *Lusitania*.

Laois, County Situated in the province of *Leinster* in the Republic of Ireland, it was formerly known as Queen's County and is part of the Midlands region. The land in the county lends itself to the agricultural industry. At the 2011 census, it had the highest population growth in the country.

ROCK OF DUNAMASE
In County Laois, the legendary home of Dermot Mac Murrough.

ROAD SIGNS
Places and names are written
in both English and Irish.

Language The Irish
language originates
from the 4th century
in the early written
language of ogham.
The language was
brought to Ireland
by the *Celts* during
the 6th century. By
the 10th century this
old Irish language
had evolved into Middle Irish, which was
spoken throughout Ireland and also in
Scotland and the Isle of Man. After the
12th century, individual languages began
to evolve: modern Irish, Scots-Gaelic and
Manx. Modern Irish went into decline during
the 18th century following restrictions
imposed during British rule, and the death
or emigration of a large proportion of Irish
speakers after *The Great Famine*.

The language was part of the Gaelic revival in the late 1800s, when efforts were made to produce Irish literature and drama, as well as to preserve traditional culture.

Irish speakers today are in a minority, apart from those living in areas known as *Gaeltachts* – places where Irish is the main language spoken. There are initiatives to keep the language alive, the main ones being the Irish language TV channel TG4 and Irish language schools called Gaelscoileanna.

KILMALKEDAR OGHAM STONE
Ogham was the first written language used in Ireland. It consisted of a series of notches carved in stone.

Larkin, James (Jim) *(1876–1947)* Labour leader and politician who is best known for promoting trade unionism in Ireland and for organising the five-month strike in 1913, for which he was imprisoned.

Late, Late Show, The Ireland's top-rated show on *RTÉ* since its inception in 1962. It involves music, chat and comedy and was presented by *Gay Byrne* for over 35 years. Currently presented by Ryan Tubridy.

Lavery, John *(1856–1941)* Portrait painter who was one of the *Impressionists*.

Leared, Arthur *(1822–1879)* Inventor of the binaural stethoscope, the first of its kind to listen with both ears.

Le Brocquy, Louis *(1916–2012)* Painter; he is well known for his series of *Portrait Heads* of literary figures that include *W. B. Yeats*, *Samuel Beckett* and *Seamus Heaney*.

JIM LARKIN
Leader of the Irish Transport and General Workers' Union who organised a lockout that lasted five months and prompted others, such as James Connolly, to campaign for workers' rights.

Lee, River River that runs through the city of *Cork*. It is popular for salmon and trout fishing and produces hydroelectric power.

Legal System The native Irish legal system was the ancient Brehon law of the Celts, which was superseded by the common law system introduced by the English. Law in the Republic of Ireland is based on common law as modified by legislation and the Irish Constitution of 1937. British legislation enacted before 1921 may have the force of law in the Republic, unless subsequently repealed by the Irish legislature.

Leinster Eastern province of the Republic of Ireland incorporating the counties of *Wexford*, *Wicklow*, *Meath*, *Westmeath*, *Longford*, *Dublin*, *Carlow*, *Kildare*, *Kilkenny*, *Offaly*, *Laois* and *Louth*.

Leitrim, County County in the north-west of the Republic of Ireland. Its land is both mountainous and heavy-soiled, and it is home to *Lough Allen*.

GLENCAR WATERFALL
A feature of County Leitrim.

RIVER LEE
As it flows through
the city of Cork.

SEÁN LEMASS
He believed in
a united Ireland.

LEPRECHAUN
A popular feature
of Irish folklore.

Lemass, Seán *(1899–1971) Fianna Fáil* politician who fought in the *Easter Rising* and was a loyal follower of *Éamon de Valera*. He was an active member of the *IRA* and rejected the *Anglo-Irish Treaty* of 1921. He was appointed Tánaiste in 1945 and succeeded de Valera as *Taoiseach* in 1959; he believed a united Ireland could be achieved peacefully through economic progress.

Leprechaun A fairy shoemaker that features in Irish *folklore*. Leprechauns know the whereabouts of hidden treasure. Legend has it that if you catch a leprechaun, he must tell you where the treasure is. However, he will try to trick you by making you look away, at which point he will vanish!

Letterkenny Town in *County Donegal*. It used to host a famous international folk festival and is adjacent to the Grianan of Aileach stone fort.

Liffey, River River that rises in the Wicklow mountains and flows through the centre of Dublin city, where it is crossed by many pedestrian and vehicular bridges.

Lifford, town Town in *County Donegal*; it is situated on the River Foyle.

Limerick, County Situated in the north of the province of *Munster*. It is known for beautiful landscapes and features flocks of migrating birds. It is home to *Lough Gur* and has archaeological remains from over 5,000 years ago.

Limerick, City Sitting at the head of the Shannon estuary, it was originally a *Viking* settlement. It is home to Limerick Castle, which was a 12th-century Norman stronghold. The town is divided into three areas: English Town, Irish Town and Newton Perry, the latter being the home of the business district.

Lismore Castle In *County Waterford*. Built on the site of the 7th century Lismore Abbey, it is owned by the Duke of Devonshire.

ADARE VILLAGE
In County Limerick contains many beautiful, traditional thatched cottages.

LIMERICK CITY
The lights of the city over the River Shannon.

Literature The earliest Irish literature that we know of originates from the 6th century in the form of poetry. Since then the language developed, but poetry remained the main vehicle of literary expression – the subject matter was vast, ranging from nature to religion to emotions. After the Norman invasions in the 12th century, *folklore* and hero-tales became more popular and were written down.

GULLIVER'S TRAVELS
Allegorical novel in which Swift examines the discrepancy between what man thinks he is and how he acts.

As English control grew stronger in Ireland, its literary traditions were taken on. However, some older Irish literary culture survived and was revived during the 18th century. *The Great Famine* led to the further decline of the Irish language and very few people were literate during these times.

An English-speaking middle class emerged in Ireland and with it came the Anglo-Irish literary tradition. *Jonathan Swift* was Ireland's first significant writer in the English language; he was followed by *Maria Edgeworth* and *William Carleton*. Many stories focused on the lives of Irish peasants. *Bram Stoker*, the author of *Dracula*, broke the traditions of the time. *Oscar Wilde* came along at the end of the 19th century with a host of popular and humorous plays and stories. The growth of nationalism towards the end of the 19th century saw a Gaelic revival epitomised in the early poetry of *W. B. Yeats*. Modern Irish literature saw the emergence of the famous figures of *James Joyce* and *Samuel Beckett*. Poetry was still a strong tradition and its popularity was reflected in the work of *Seamus Heaney* and *Patrick Kavanagh*. Much 19th- and 20th-century literature reflects the political situation in Ireland and many writers from lower social classes became popular.

BRAM STOKER
Popular Irish writer who wrote *Dracula*.

DAVID LLOYD GEORGE
British Prime Minister; he played a large part in Irish politics during the early 1900s.

Lloyd George, David *(1863–1945)* British Prime Minister during the time of the *Anglo-Irish Treaty*.

Loftus, Adam *(c.1533–1606)* Former archbishop of Dublin and first provost of *Trinity College Dublin*, founded in 1592.

Londonderry – See *Derry*

Longford, County County in the Republic of Ireland; its south-western borders are formed by the *River Shannon* and Lough Ree. Its low-lying land makes it favourable for *agriculture*.

Lonsdale, Kathleen *(1903–1971)* Scientist known for her work on the structures of organic molecules using X-ray photography to investigate the texture of crystals, including bladder and kidney stones. In 1968, she became the first female president of the British Association for the Advancement of Science.

PHIL LYNOTT
The lead singer of Thin Lizzy.

Louth, County The smallest county in the Republic of Ireland. It is separated from Northern Ireland by Carlingford Lough. Its other borders are formed by the *Irish Sea* to the east and the *River Boyne* to the south. Louth boasts the monastic sites of Monasterboice and Mellifont.

Lynch, Jack *(1917–1999)* Leader of *Fianna Fáil* and *Taoiseach* from 1966–73 and again from 1977–79. He played a major part in stabilizing the country during the *Troubles.*

Lynott, Phil *(1949–1986)* Musician who was frontman of the band *Thin Lizzy*; he also had success as a solo artist. His distinctive vocals and bass guitar riffs were a big part of Thin Lizzy's success. He struggled with drug and alcohol addiction, which led to his early death at the age of 36. There is a statue of him on Harry Street in *Dublin*.

M

HENRY II
The first English king to set foot in Ireland.

MacBride, Seán *(1904–1988)* Politician and peace campaigner involved with the *IRA* as director of intelligence and chief of staff. He resigned from the IRA after the 1937 enactment of the Irish Constitution. As a rights campaigner, he worked with Amnesty International and was awarded the Nobel Peace Prize in 1974.

MacGillycuddy's Reeks A mountain range in *County Kerry*. The range includes *Carrantuohill*, which is the highest peak in Ireland.

MacMurrough, Dermot *(1110–1171)* High King of Ireland and King of *Leinster*, who promised his daughter to Richard de Clare (*Strongbow*). He formed ties with King Henry II and is often seen as a traitor who invited the English invasion of Ireland.

Malahide Castle 12th-century Norman stronghold, it lies just north of *Dublin*. The grounds of the castle were opened as a venue for concerts in 2007 and the likes of the Arctic Monkeys, Radiohead and Eric Clapton have played there.

Markievicz, Constance Georgina, Countess *(1868–1927)* Republican activist who fought in the *Easter Rising*, commanding 120 soldiers. Before that she joined *Sinn Féin*, founded the Republican Youth organisation and became honorary president of the Irish Women's Workers' Union. She was the first woman to be elected to the British House of Commons in 1918, though she did not take her seat. In 1919 she became the first Irish female cabinet minister and the second female government minister in Europe.

Martin, James *(1893–1981)* Aeronautical engineer. He is known for designing ejection seats for pilots, as well as a three-wheeled car and fighter jets.

MALAHIDE CASTLE
One of the best-preserved Norman fortresses in Ireland.

COUNTY MAYO
The lakes of County Mayo are famous for fishing.

MARY MCALEESE
The first president to have come from Northern Ireland.

Mayo, County County in the Republic of Ireland, it is situated on the Atlantic coast. The pilgrimage sites of *Croagh Patrick* and *Knock* are both in this county, as are many ancient archaeological sites that date back to the Neolithic period. *Achill Island* lies just off the coast of County Mayo.

McAleese, Mary *(1951–)* The eighth president of the Republic of Ireland. She is also the first president to have come from Northern Ireland.

McAliskey, Bernadette *(1947–)* Born Bernadette Devlin, she is a Republican activist. At the age of 21 she became the youngest woman ever to have been elected to the British parliament. She was arrested for leading Catholic rioters in 1969 and survived an assassination attempt in 1981 after she openly supported the *hunger strikes*. She was suspended from parliament in 1972 for punching a politician who said that 'the soldiers who took part in *Bloody Sunday* only fired in self-defence'.

McCourt, Frank *(1930–2009)* Author best known for his Pulitzer Prize-winning memoir of growing up in Limerick, *Angela's Ashes* (1996), which was later made into a film. His brothers are also writers and have produced a stage show about their lives.

McGrath, Paul *(1959–)* Footballer who played for Aston Villa and Manchester United. He also played for the Republic of Ireland national team from 1985–97.

Meaney, Colm *(1953–)* Actor best known for his role as Chief Miles O'Brien in the *Star Trek* television series. His first TV appearance was in *Z-Cars* in 1978. He moved to New York in 1982 and he now stars in *Hell on Wheels*, which premiered in November 2011.

Meath, County Situated in the province of *Leinster* in the Republic of Ireland. It is home to the Hill of Tara – coronation site of the ancient kings of Ireland – *Bective Abbey*, Trim Castle and also the town of Kells, which is associated with the *Book of Kells*.

FRANK MCCOURT
Best remembered for his memoir, *Angela's Ashes*.

COUNTY MEATH
Ruins of a monastery on the Hill of Slane.

M

MEGALITHS
A common feature of ancient Irish archaeology.

CLIFFS OF MOHER
They are often regarded as a natural wonder of the world.

Megalith A large stone that has been used to make a monument, either on its own or together with other large stones, such as Stonehenge in England. The majority of megalithic tombs were constructed in the Neolithic period. Many Irish megalithic tombs were passage or portal tombs, such as Poulnabrone, Clooneen Wedge and the Legananny Dolmen. It may be that they have a symbolic significance as well as being used to house the remains of the dead. Many megalithic structures, such as *Newgrange* tomb, display evidence of astronomical alignment.

Moher, Cliffs of Cliffs formed out of dark sandstone and topped with black shale. They are situated in *County Clare*, at the edge of *The Burren*, overlooking the *Aran Islands*. The cliffs are considered one of the natural wonders of the world. The spectacular views from the cliff edges attract nearly 1 million visitors every year.

Monaghan, County Situated in *Ulster* in the Republic of Ireland, it is a low-lying county characterised by the 'basket of eggs' topography of drumlins.

Monaghan, town An agricultural town in *County Monaghan*. It is home to a popular fishing centre and a Gothic-style cathedral.

Monasteries Monastic life became widespread throughout the 5th century. The monasteries became centres for learning and produced works of art, and invaders such as the *Vikings* were attracted to their wealth.

MONASTERY
After Henry VIII's dissolution of the monasteries, monastic life went into decline, along with the educational and health services they provided.

Following the Norman invasion, monasteries became more structured and divided by order, such as Cistercian, Dominican and Franciscan.

After Henry VIII's dissolution of the monasteries, monastic life went into decline. Some orders survived, although entry into monastic life became quite rare during the late 20th and early 21st centuries.

Monuments

POULNABRONE DOLMEN

BUNRATTY CASTLE

DROMORE CASTLE

HIGH CROSSES

ROSS CASTLE

DROMBEG STONE CIRCLE

KELLS PRIORY

ROCKFLEET CASTLE

CLONMACNOISE

Moore, Christy *(1945–)* Folk singer who is noted for performing with a guitar and a bodhrán (an Irish frame drum). His songs are often on the subject of social and political issues.

Morrison, Van *(1945–)* Musician best known for his hit singles, 'Moondance' and 'Brown Eyed Girl'. He started with the band Them – their most popular song was 'Gloria'. He built a strong reputation with critically acclaimed albums; his style is often referred to as Celtic Soul.

Mountjoy Castle Early 17th-century castle built on the shores of *Lough Neagh*. It was fought over by the English and Irish many times during the following 100 years.

Mountains of Mourne A mountain range mostly made of granite, situated in the south of *County Down*.

VAN MORRISON
Has won six Grammy Awards during his career to date.

MOUNTAINS OF MOURNE
An area of outstanding beauty receiving visitors all year round.

Mount Sandel The oldest archaeological site in Ireland. It dates back to the Mesolithic Age, which is the time when settlers first appeared in Ireland following the Ice Age. The site contains the remains of a number of small huts that are believed to be the remnants of the earliest human settlement in Ireland.

Mullingar, town Situated in the county of *Westmeath*, it was an important stopping place on road and railway links. It also had a harbour on the Royal Canal – a waterway that linked *Dublin* to the *River Shannon*.

MUNSTER

A scenic vignette of Queenstown and Cobh.

Munster Southern province of the Republic of Ireland, it incorporates the counties of *Cork, Clare*, *Kerry*, *Limerick*, *Tipperary* and *Waterford*. In the 12th century it was divided into the Kingdoms of Thomond, Desmond and Ormonde.

Munster Plantation A period of rapid English colonisation where native land was confiscated and redistributed amongst the English settlers.

M

IRISH MUSEUMS

Name	Location	Description
The National Gallery of Ireland	Dublin	Collection of European art from the 14th to the 20th-century covering all major schools.
The Irish Museum of Modern Art	Dublin	Permanent collection plus exhibitions of modern and contemporary art, featuring visual and performance crossovers.
Wexford County Museum	Wexford	Housed in a 13th-century Norman castle, it has a wide range of local historical items.
The Hunt Museum	Limerick	Private collection and temporary exhibitions.
National Museum of Ireland	Dublin	Artefacts dating from 7000 BC to modern times, plus guest exhibitions.

DIVISIONS OF THE NATIONAL MUSEUM OF IRELAND

Name	Location	Description
Collins Barracks	Dublin	Decorative Arts and History.
Turlough Park	County Mayo	Country Life
Merrion Street	Dublin	Natural History

NATIONAL MUSEUMS OF NORTHERN IRELAND

Name	Location	Description
Ulster Museum	Belfast	Rich in archaeology, art and history and a feature on Belfast's recent past.
Ulster Folk & Transport Museum	Cultra	Early 20th-century Ulster
Ulster American Folk Park	Omagh	The story of emigration.
Armagh County Museum	Armagh	The oldest county museum in Ireland, with artefacts from prehistoric times through to the 19th century, plus special exhibitions.

THE BODHRÁN
Is thought to have
been introduced to
Ireland by the Celts
and was originally
used during battles.
It is made from goat
skin stretched over a
wooden frame and is
played with a double
ended stick, called a
cipín. Bodhrán frames
are often decorated
with Celtic designs.

Music From the 10th century onwards the
Irish annals list native musicians, though
the earliest written music dates from the
1700s. The *harp* was introduced in the 10th
century and became the national instrument
of Ireland. In the 12th century harpists were
often accompanied by a bodhrán. Other
traditional folk instruments were developed
later, one of the most important being the
fiddle. Uileann pipes (similar to Scottish
bagpipes) developed in the early 18th century,
followed by flutes, whistles and the accordion
during the 19th century. Banjos, mandolins
and guitars appeared in the 20th century.
Traditional Irish music was mainly dance
music, the most famous forms being the reel,
the hornpipe and the jig – a jig is often written
in 6/8, 9/8 or 12/8 time, which gives it its
distinctive feel. As well as dance music, Irish
folk tunes were written as vocal pieces, many

of which had come as stories and rhymes from the older language tradition. There are also the caoineadh, which are laments – the subject matter for many of these songs is often the fate of Irish emigrants and, more recently, the *Troubles* in Northern Ireland.

Many Irish musicians have found success in the modern music world by using traditional Irish techniques with modern rock and pop styles, most notably *Van Morrison*, *Sinéad O'Connor* and *Enya*. The Pogues famously fused traditional music with punk rock and, more recently, the multi-award winning band The Script has found international success.

IRISH MUSICIANS
Playing traditional instruments: guitar, banjo and fiddle.

Murdoch, Iris *(1919–1999)* Born in Dublin, daughter of a civil servant, she gained a First in Mods and Greats from Oxford and published her first novel, *Under the Net*, in 1954. She was famous as a prolific author of novels on philosophical themes before she was diagnosed with Alzheimer's in 1997.

Murray, Ann *(1949–)* Mezzo-soprano from Dublin, she has performed as a soloist both nationally and internationally. She mainly performs with the English National Opera at Covent Garden, London. In 2002, she was made a Dame of the British Empire.

MUSSENDEN TEMPLE
The erosion of the cliff face by the sea has brought the temple closer and closer to the cliff edge.

Mussenden Temple
A small, circular building that was an 18th-century temple. It is built on the ruins of Downhill Castle on the cliffs of Castlerock, *County Derry*.

M

THE STONE OF DESTINY
Also known as Lia Fáil, is said to have been brought to Ireland by the semi-divine race known as the Tuatha Dé Danann. It is at the Hill of Tara in County Meath.

Mythology The mythological origins of Ireland stem from an epic battle for control between the Fomorians, who represent the gods of chaos and nature, and the Tuatha Dé Danann, who represent human civilisation and the goddess Danu. Legend has it that the tribes of the Tuatha Dé Danann moved to 'the Land of Eternal Youth', whilst the Fomorians withdrew to an underground world to rule over the fairies – thus leaving Ireland to mortals. The chronicles of these epic battles are retold in hero-tales, such as the stories of *Cú Chulainn*.

Mythological Cycle The stories of the legendary kings of Ireland, such as *Cormac Mac Airt*. It was the duty of court poets to record and recount the history of the king they served; to make them more interesting, the stories were often mixed with Irish *mythology*.

Naas, town Town in *County Kildare*, just south of *Dublin*. It is best known for its agricultural and manufacturing industries, and for its racecourse.

National Botanic Gardens Founded in 1795, the gardens span over 50 acres of land. The gardens contain collections of rare and exotic plants. The Palm House and curvilinear range of glasshouses were completed by Richard Turner in 1848.

NATIONAL BOTANIC GARDENS
Are located just north-west of Dublin's city centre.

National Gallery of Ireland (NGI) Founded in 1864 in Dublin, the gallery houses collections of national and European art, including: 14,000 artworks, 2,500 oil paintings, 5,000 drawings and 5,000 prints, as well as sculptures, furniture, historical artefacts and installations.

Nationalist Party (Northern Ireland) Political party founded after *partition* in 1921. The party was set up to represent Catholics within politics. It faded away during the 1960s when it failed to fall in line with the civil rights movements of the time and was superseded by the *SDLP*.

National University of Ireland Founded under the 1908 Irish Universities Act. The aim was to make higher education readily available to Catholics. The constituent universities are the University Colleges of Dublin, Cork, Galway and Maynooth. There are also five recognised colleges of the NUI.

UNIVERSITY COLLEGE GALWAY
One of the four universities that form part of the National University of Ireland.

LOUGH NEAGH
The most famous legend of its origin is that the giant, Finn mac Cumhaill, scooped up a piece of land and threw it towards Scotland. He missed and the clod landed in the Irish Sea, which created the Isle of Man.

LIAM NEESON
World-famous Irish actor.

Navan, town Situated in *County Meath*, it is adjacent to many ancient ruins, including *Bective Abbey*, Rathaldron Castle and the Hill of Tara.

Navan Fort A Bronze Age hill fort near *Armagh*, Northern Ireland. Archaeologists have discovered a number of circular dwellings underneath the structure that date back to around 700 BC.

Neagh, Lough Huge lake in Northern Ireland, the largest in the British Isles. There are some islands on the lake; the most famous, and largest, is Ram's Island, which houses ancient ruins and was once an RAF flying boat base.

Neeson, Liam *(1952–)* Award-winning actor whose most famous role was Oskar Schindler in Spielberg's *Schindler's List*. He has a successful Hollywood career and has starred in such films as: *Star Wars, Batman Begins, The Dark Knight Rises, Love Actually* and *Taken* and he was also the voice of Aslan in *The Chronicles of Narnia*. He was awarded an OBE in 1999.

Neutrality The Republic of Ireland's foreign policy following the outbreak of World War II. It was only possible after British control of Irish ports was relinquished in 1938.

Newbridge House An 18th-century Georgian estate that lies just outside *Dublin*.

Newgrange One of the most famous passage tombs from the Neolithic Age. It is also linked to astronomical science due to the positioning of its entrance.

Newry, town Situated at the shores of Carlingford Lough, it was an important town in medieval times due to its location. In the 18th century it was connected to *Lough Neagh* via the first ever inland canal.

NEWBRIDGE HOUSE
Has one of the best preserved Georgian interiors in Ireland.

NEWGRANGE
One of Ireland's most famous archaeological discoveries.

Nore, River River in the Republic of Ireland that is popular for trout and salmon fishing.

Northern Ireland The part of Ireland that remains part of the UK. It is made up of the counties *Armagh*, *Antrim*, *Down*, *Fermanagh*, *Derry* and *Tyrone*. The capital of Northern Ireland is *Belfast* and one of its major tourist attractions is *The Giant's Causeway*. Northern Ireland, Belfast in particular, was the scene of the *Troubles* of the late 1960s and into the 1990s.

RIVER NORE
Parts of the river are listed as special conservation areas.

Northern Ireland Assembly Convened under the terms of the *Good Friday Agreement* of 1998, the Assembly is the governing body of *Northern Ireland*. It is made up of 108 democratically elected members (MLAs) who represent the constituencies of Northern Ireland. It sits at Parliament Buildings at *Stormont* in Belfast. One of its important purposes is to aid cooperation with the Republic of Ireland on matters of mutual interest.

Northern Ireland Peace Process Refers to the time in the 1990s when multi-party talks led to an *IRA* ceasefire and, eventually, the *Good Friday Agreement* (1998).

Norton, Graham *(1963–)* Born Graham William Walker, he is an actor and comedian best known for his chat show *The Graham Norton Show* and as the host of the *Eurovision Song Contest*, as well as other BBC and Channel 4 TV shows. He has won five BAFTA Awards for Best Entertainment Performance.

GRAHAM NORTON
Has said he often felt alienated growing up as a Protestant in the predominantly Catholic Republic of Ireland.

BRIAN BORU
The O'Brien dynasty is
descended from this
High King.

O'Brien Irish dynasty descended from *Brian Boru*. They remained strong during the Anglo-Norman invasion through a combination of negotiation and resistance. The dynasty triumphed in many political struggles and survives to this day.

O'Brien, Flann *(1911–1966)* A pseudonym of Brian O'Nolan. He wrote in Irish and English and was well known for his column in the *Irish Times*.

O'Byrne, Fiach Mac Hugh *(1534–1597)* Resistance leader during the English occupation of *County Wicklow*. He had many early successes, but was eventually captured and executed.

O'Connell, Daniel *(1775–1847)* Politician who campaigned for Catholic emancipation and for the repeal of the 1801 *Act of Union* between Britain and Ireland.

O'Connor of Connacht Irish dynasty dating from the 11th century. King Rory O'Connor was the man responsible for angering *Dermot MacMurrough*, who invited support from the English in order to regain his throne.

O'Donnell, Daniel *(1961–)* Singer and TV presenter who found fame in the 1980s with his self-funded first single 'My Donegal Shore'. He has had a long career topping the charts in the UK, Ireland and North America and was awarded an honorary MBE in 2002.

Ó Faoláin, Seán *(1900–1991)* Writer from *County Cork*. He is best known for his biographies of *Daniel O'Connell* and *Éamon de Valera*, whom he'd fought alongside in the *IRA*.

DANIEL O'CONNELL
Became a champion of Catholic emancipation.

STATUE
Of Daniel O'Connell at the end of O'Connell Street in Dublin.

CLONMACNOISE
In County Offaly is the most
famous monastic ruin in Ireland.

LIAM O'FLAHERTY
A significant Irish novelist.

Offaly, County County in the Republic of Ireland. The area is well known for its ancient Christian remains, the most famous being *Clonmacnoise*.

O'Flaherty, Liam *(1896–1984)* Writer from the *Aran Islands* who is best known for his short stories set in *Dublin*. His 1925 work, *The Informer*, which still achieves good sales, was made into a Hollywood movie.

O'Hanlon, Ardal *(1965–)* Actor best known for his role as Father Dougal McGuire in the Channel 4 TV show, *Father Ted*. He has since starred in other sitcoms, including *My Hero* and *Blessed*; he has also appeared in *Doctor Who* and several *RTÉ* television series. O'Hanlon's novel, *Talk of the Town* (published as *Knick Knack Paddy Whack* in the US), was published in 1999.

O'Hara, Maureen *(1920–2015)* Actor who appeared in more than 50 Hollywood films, including: *Jamaica Inn, The Black Swan, The Parent Trap* and *Rio Grande*. She often starred alongside John Wayne. In 2004, she released her autobiography, *'Tis Herself,* which became a *New York Times* bestseller. In the same year she was also awarded a Lifetime Achievement Award by the Irish Film and Television Academy. In 2011 she was formally inducted into the Irish American Hall of Fame.

O'Higgins, Kevin *(1892–1927)* Revolutionary and then politician at the foundation of the *Irish Free State.* A strong supporter of the *Anglo-Irish Treaty,* he was Minister for Justice and authorized stern action against the *IRA,* which resulted in his assassination in 1927.

Oireachtas The name given to the parliament of the Republic of Ireland – it consists of *Dáil Éireann* and *Seanad Éireann*.

LOGO
Of the Oireachtas.

O'Leary, Michael *(1961–)* CEO of the airline *Ryanair*, he is one of the wealthiest businessmen in the Republic of Ireland.

Omagh, town Town in *County Tyrone* that was the scene of a Republican terrorist attack in 1998 when a car bomb exploded, killing 29 people. The *Real IRA* claimed responsibility for the attack. The attack motivated parties towards further peace talks in Northern Ireland and led to a permanent ceasefire for the Real IRA. Omagh is also a popular tourist destination and its waterways are an attraction for many fishermen.

MICHAEL O'LEARY
Following the success of Ryanair, he is now one of the wealthiest people in Ireland.

OMAGH MEMORIAL GARDEN
Built to remember all of those who died during the Omagh car bomb attack.

O'Malley, Donogh *(1921–1968)* Politician with *Fianna Fáil*. He served as Minister for Health from 1965–66 and as Minister for Education from 1966–68. He is best known for introducing free secondary education for all in 1967. He also introduced means-tested grants for university education, making higher education available to those from poorer backgrounds. His education reforms made him one of the most popular and well-respected members of government.

O'Neill, Hugh *(1550–1616)* Ulster rebel who became the second Earl of Tyrone. He grew up in *The English Pale* and spent much of his life attempting to extend his authority over the Ulster lords, whilst supporting English tax policies. He overstretched his resources and was defeated in his rebellion against the government in 1601 in Kinsale, *County Cork*. He fled the country and, although his jubilant return was expected, he died in exile in Italy.

HUGH O'NEILL
His failed rebellion proved to be the last great uprising of the old Irish chieftains.

PEEP O'DAY BOYS
Later became known as the Orange Order.

ORANGE ORDER FLAG
Features the English cross and the purple Williamite star.

Orange Order Protestant organisation set up in 1795 as a response to the Catholic *Defenders*. They commemorate William III's victory at the *Battle of the Boyne* every year during the Orange Order parade. The Orange Order has a history of clashes with Catholic societies, such as their involvement in the *Rebellion of 1798* and the Catholic emancipation movement. 'Orangeism' became popular with English landlords who opposed *Home Rule* and again in 1921 with the formation of Northern Ireland. There is some Nationalist opposition to the order, particularly regarding the route of some of their traditional marches.

Orangemen The term used to describe members of the *Orange Order*, who dress in black suits, with an orange sash, white gloves, an umbrella and a bowler hat. Orangemen march in Orange Order parades; the orange of the sash is in honour of King William III (William of Orange).

O'Reilly, Tony *(1936–)* Former international rugby player, he became a businessman in 1973. He is noted for his involvement with the Independent News & Media Group and was the CEO of H. J. Heinz Company. He was Ireland's first billionaire.

H. J. HEINZ
Where Tony O'Reilly served as CEO of the company.

Osborne, Walter *(1859–1903)* Painter influenced by the *Impressionists*, he is most famous for his portrait and landscape paintings. He studied and worked all over Europe, most notably in Belgium, France and England.

O'Toole, Peter *(1932–2013)* Actor best known for his role as T. E. Lawrence in *Lawrence of Arabia*. He won many awards, and although he received eight nominations, he has never won an Academy Award. In recognition of his work, he received an honorary Academy Award in 2003 for his lifetime achievement.

P

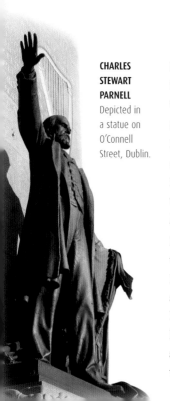

CHARLES STEWART PARNELL
Depicted in a statue on O'Connell Street, Dublin.

Paisley, Ian *(1926–2014)* Politician and leader of the *DUP* from 1971–2008. He opposed the *Good Friday Agreement,* but later went into government with *Sinn Féin*.

Pale, The English The name given to an area around *County Dublin* that was taken over by English settlers in 1171. The medieval boundaries were recognised politically for centuries, until the *Plantation* of Ireland in 1556.

Parnell, Charles Stewart *(1846–1891)* Politician who became leader of the Irish Parliamentary Party, which split following revelations surrounding his affair with a married woman. He campaigned for land reforms and *Home Rule*. His reputation was marred by accusations of sympathy with the *Phoenix Park* murderers but he was later vindicated by the Parnell commission.

Partition The division of Ireland into *Northern Ireland* and the *Irish Free State* (later known as the Republic of Ireland) in 1920. The 1937 constitution laid claim to the six counties of Northern Ireland until after the *Good Friday Agreement* of 1998.

Passage East An ancient *Viking* settlement from the 10th century, situated in *County Waterford*. It was also home to Geneva Barracks, a British Army base during the *Rebellion of 1798*.

Patrick, Saint The patron saint of Ireland. His feast day is on 17 March. *St Patrick's Day* is celebrated internationally, partly due to the Irish *diaspora* and the drinking tradition that goes with it. St Patrick is responsible for introducing Christianity to Ireland during the 5th century. Legend has it that he heard the voice of God telling him to return to Ireland and spread the Christian faith.

ST PATRICK
The patron saint of Ireland, he is responsible for introducing Christianity to the country during the 5th century.

P

PEAT
When dried, peat can be used as a fuel.

PENAL LAWS
Friars bribed mayors with alcohol so that they wouldn't be expelled from their positions.

Pearse, Patrick (Pádraig) Henry *(1879–1916)* Revolutionary and activist who was a founding member of the *Irish Volunteers*. As commander-in-chief of the Volunteers, he read aloud the Proclamation of Independence, to which he was a signatory, during the 1916 *Easter Rising*. He was executed for his involvement in the Rising.

Peat Bogs Waterlogged areas of land grow a thick blanket of moss called peat. When dried, peat can be burnt as fuel, or used to enrich soil; this knowledge led to the mass extraction of Ireland's peat during the 1940s. The Bog of Allen is the country's main source of peat today.

Penal Laws A series of laws enacted in the 1690s under the Protestant King William that directly discriminated against Roman Catholics. Under the laws, Catholic clergy could not fight and they could not be educated abroad; Catholics could not buy land, or inherit land from a Protestant, and Catholic landowners had to divide their land between their own male heirs.

Phoenix Park Murders (1882) Assassination carried out by a splinter group of the *Irish Republican Brotherhood*. Lord Cavendish, the newly appointed chief secretary of Ireland, and his under-secretary were both stabbed to death.

LORD CAVENDISH
And his under-secretary, Thomas Burke, were murdered by the Invincibles.

Place Names Many Irish place names derive from the Irish language names:

- Bally, meaning 'home': Ballymena, Ballyclare

- Carrig, meaning 'rock': *Carrickfergus*, Carrigaline

- Drohid, meaning 'bridge': *Drogheda*, Clondrohid

- Ennis, meaning 'island': *Enniskillen*

- Port, meaning 'stronghold': *Portlaoise*, Portadown

- Knock, meaning 'hill': *Knock*, Knockcloghrim.

Some are two words joined together, such as Ballynoe (Bally meaning 'home' and Noe meaning 'new').

Some are of Norse origin, brought over with the Vikings:

- *Wicklow* - *Víkinga-lág* – meaning 'Vikings' Low Place'

- Fastnet - *Hvasstann-ait* – meaning 'Windy Tooth'

- Leixlip - *Lax Hlaup* – meaning 'Salmon Leap'.

Plantation The name given to the colonisation of Ireland by English and Scottish settlers between 1556 and 1660. It formed part of Tudor policy to reassert English influence in Ireland. Catholic loyalists put up strong resistance, but were later crushed by Oliver Cromwell in 1649. Much of the land was taken from Irish Catholics and distributed to English soldiers and noblemen.

ST MICHAEL'S CHURCH
A typical example of the plantation churches built in Ireland during the 16th and 17th centuries.

Plunkett, Joseph Mary *(1887–1916)* Revolutionary who was a member of the *Irish Volunteers* and the *Irish Republican Brotherhood*. He travelled to Germany with *Roger Casement* to rally for support and military aid. He was executed for his part in the *Easter Rising* of 1916.

Political Parties The people of both Northern Ireland and the Republic of Ireland are represented by many political parties. The main ones are:

POLITICAL PARTIES – REPUBLIC OF IRELAND

Party	Leader	Founded	Founded by	Position
Fine Gael	Enda Kenny	1933	Eoin O'Duffy	Centre-right
Labour Party	Joan Burton	1912	James Connolly/James Larkin	Centre-left
Fianna Fáil	Micheál Martin	1926	Éamon de Valera	Centre
Sinn Féin	Gerry Adams	1905	Arthur Griffith	Left
Socialist Party	Collective	1996	Joe Higgins	Far-left
Green Party	Eamon Ryan	1981	none	Centre-left

POLITICAL PARTIES – NORTHERN IRELAND

Party	Leader	Founded	Founded by	Position
Sinn Féin	Gerry Adams	1905	Arthur Griffith	Left
Democratic Unionist Party (DUP)	Peter Robinson	1971	Ian Paisley	Centre-right
Ulster Unionist Party (UUP)	Mike Nesbitt	1905	Edward Carson	Centre-right
Social Democratic and Labour Party (SDLP)	Colum Eastwood	1970	Ivan Cooper, Gerry Fitt, Paddy Devlin, John Hume	Centre-left

MARCHING BANDS
Are an old tradition
in Ulster.

IRISH JEWISH MUSEUM
In Dublin.

Popular Culture Modern Irish culture is built on the traditions of the past in the areas of *language*, *literature*, *music* and *history*. Traditional ways of life can still be found in rural areas today, in some of which people still speak Irish as their first language. Ireland does not have an official religion and although many people are Christian, other *religions* are also represented.

Modern Irish music developed during the 1960s with the emergence of rock, pop and punk. The most notable Irish bands and musicians are *Thin Lizzy*, *Van Morrison*, *Enya*, *Sinead O'Connor*, *The Corrs*, *Boyzone*, *Westlife* and *U2*. Traditional music is still celebrated and practised. Irish step dancing remains popular and was revived in the 1990s by *Riverdance*.

Pub culture has grown in the last century and Ireland is famous for its *Guinness*, *whiskey* and nightlife. Although Irish *food* is still celebrated, it has been somewhat taken over by fast food.

Portlaoise A town in *County Laois*, close to *Dublin*. It is most famous for the ruins of a castle that belonged to *Dermot MacMurrough*.

Potato Blight A disease that causes the potato crop to rot whilst in the ground, making the potato inedible. It was the cause of *The Great Famine*, which lasted from 1845–52.

Poteen A very strong alcoholic drink made from potatoes. It was banned by the English in 1661 and despite being legalised for mass production in 1997, many still prefer the prohibited version.

POTATO BLIGHT
Was brought to Ireland from Europe and North America.

Price, Dorothy *(1890–1954)* Dublin-based paediatrician who is best remembered for contributing to the elimination of tuberculosis in Ireland by campaigning, over many years, for a vaccination programme.

BRIGHTON BOMBING (1984)
The bomb was planted by Provisional Irish Republican Army (IRA) member Patrick Magee, with the intention of assassinating Prime Minister Margaret Thatcher.

IRISH PUBS
Often have a distinctive look.

Provisional IRA In 1969 the *IRA* split into the Provisional and Official IRA. The Provisionals made up the violent wing of the organisation which was a prominent force during the *Troubles* of the 1970s. They were responsible for the infamous bombing of the Grand Hotel in Brighton during the Conservative Party conference in 1984.

Pubs Public houses, places where alcohol is sold, serve as a meeting place for Irish communities. Many Irish pubs are now tourist attractions, particularly in big cities and tourist towns. Irish pubs are not tied, and will usually bear the name of the current or previous owner.

Punchestown Racecourse in *County Kildare* near the town of *Naas*. It is home to the Punchestown International Horse Trials in May each year.

Punt The name given to the Irish pound. It was the currency of the Republic of Ireland and was superseded by the euro in 2002.

Quinn, Aidan *(1959–)* American actor who spent much of his life in *County Offaly*. He has starred in many Hollywood films, including *Unknown* alongside *Liam Neeson*.

Quinn, Edel *(1907–1944)* Missionary who devoted her life to helping the poor and sick people of *Dublin*. She went on to be a missionary in Africa before dying of tuberculosis. She was put forward for beatification (the third of four steps to being canonised) in 1956; in 1994 she was declared 'venerable' (meaning a heroic and virtuous servant of God) by Pope John Paul II. The campaign for her beatification continues.

EDEL QUINN
Devoted her life to helping the poor and sick, both in Ireland and in Africa.

R

SIR WALTER RALEIGH
Was given land in Munster by
Queen Elizabeth I following
the Plantation of Munster.

Raleigh, Walter *(1554–1618)* English explorer
who is said to have introduced the potato to
Ireland. He was favoured by Queen Elizabeth I;
he received a large estate during the *Plantation
of Munster*. He sold his land to *Richard Boyle*
in 1602 after many difficulties and disputes.

Rathlin Island Island off the north coast of
County Antrim. It was where Robert the Bruce
sought refuge in 1306. It has been occupied
by the *Vikings* and the Scots, but its ownership
is now Irish.

Real IRA An extremist wing of the *IRA*
that splintered from the main group in 1997.
It was responsible for the *Omagh bombing*
in 1998, which killed 28 people.

Rebellion of 1798 An unsuccessful Nationalist uprising against English rule in Ireland, influenced by the events of the French Revolution. It was propelled by the Society of *United Irishmen*, but uncoordinated attacks and the strategic arrest of their leaders resulted in a huge death toll.

VINEGAR HILL
Near Wexford, it was the scene of a bloody battle in 1798.

IRISH FREEDOM FIGHTER
Depicted by a statue in Wexford.

Recycling The Irish Environmental Protection Agency is responsible for recycling in Ireland and although it trails behind other European countries, Ireland's recycling did increase during the late 20th and early 21st centuries. Today, almost 30 per cent of household waste is recycled.

Redmond, John Edward *(1856–1918)* Nationalist politician who campaigned for *Home Rule* in Ireland. His condemnation of the *Easter Rising* ruined his reputation among Irish Nationalists.

COBH CATHEDRAL
St Colman's Cathedral, begun in 1868 and completed in 1915.

Religion Ireland has been a Christian country since the arrival of *St Patrick* in the 5th century. The main religion in the Republic of Ireland today is Christianity, with the largest Church being the Catholic Church. The Republic of Ireland does, however, have a secular government; the majority of the population class themselves as Catholic, although the percentage of those attending mass has decreased dramatically since the 1970s. Although a small minority are Protestant, Irish Christianity is dominated by Catholicism. When English Protestants came to settle in Ireland and introduced the *Penal Laws*, this caused great tension between Catholics, who were generally Nationalists and wanted Ireland (and Northern Ireland) to be run as a republic, and Protestants, who were usually Unionists and wanted Ireland to be part of the United Kingdom.

In Northern Ireland, whilst the main religion is still Christianity and the largest single Church is the Catholic Church, there are more Protestants and Anglicans overall. The Catholic (Nationalist) and Protestant (Unionist) divide was most noticeable in Northern Ireland, particularly during the era of the *Troubles*, when violence and terrorism broke out between the two communities over the constitutional status of Northern Ireland.

Both countries have a small representation of other faiths, including Islam, Judaism, Bahá'i, Hinduism, Sikhism and Buddhism, as well as a growing atheist population.

CHRISTIANITY

Is the main religion in both Northern Ireland and the Republic of Ireland, although the divide between Protestant and Catholic denominations has caused many conflicts in the past.

R

Republicanism The general term given to the underlying philosophy of various organisations who were, or are, willing to use force to achieve their goals. Republican groups range from the *United Irishmen* of the 1790s, through to the *IRA* of the late 20th century. Republicans aim to achieve an Irish republic, free of English rule. Many Republican groups have sought to effect change through rebellions and terrorist attacks, such as the *Rebellion of 1798*, the *Easter Rising* (1916) and the *Troubles*. Extreme Republican groups, such as the *Real IRA* and the *Provisional IRA* have been responsible for many terrible terrorist attacks during the late 20th century.

Riverdance Irish dancing show that was brought to an international audience during the 1994 *Eurovision Song Contest*. It was spearheaded by champion dancer *Michael Flatley,* and its initial success led to a full-length stage show, which then evolved into three different companies touring the world.

RIVERDANCE
Was responsible for the international revival of Irish step dancing.

Robinson, Mary *(1944–)* The seventh president, and first female president, of Ireland (from 1990–97). She campaigned for the liberalisation of Ireland's laws, particularly regarding divorce, abortion and equality.

Roche, Adi *(1957–)* Campaigner for human rights and CEO of the charity Chernobyl Children's Project International. She has received several awards for her humanitarian efforts and has raised over €80 million to date.

Roche, Stephen *(1959–)* Professional road cyclist who became the second person ever to win the Triple Crown: the Tour de France, the Giro d'Italia and the World Road Race Championship. His son, Nicolas Roche, is now a professional road-race cyclist, too; he rides for the team AG2R-La Mondiale and has represented Ireland at the Olympics and World Championships.

Roscommon Castle 13th-century castle that was held by the kings of Connacht.

STEPHEN ROCHE
Competing in the Tour
de France, 1993.

ROSCOMMON CASTLE
13th-century stronghold of
the kings of Connacht.

Rothe House One of the earliest country houses in Ireland, it is situated in *County Kilkenny*. It now houses a collection of *Charles Stewart Parnell* memorabilia.

Round Towers Free-standing stone towers built by Irish monks during the 10th–14th centuries. The entrance was often placed about 10 ft (3 m) off the ground, so that the monks could protect their valuables from the invading *Vikings*.

Royal Irish Academy (**RIA**) Institution founded in 1785 to promote science, literature and antiquities, as well as other academic fields. It publishes many academic papers and was once home to research laboratories.

RTÉ The abbreviation for Radio Teilifís Éireann – Radio and Television of Ireland. It is a public service broadcaster funded via licence fees and advertising. It was established in 1961, which makes it one of the oldest broadcasters in the world.

ROUND TOWERS
The doors were deliberately placed high off the ground, as a defence against raiding Viking warriors.

Rugby Rugby has been played in Ireland since the mid 19th century, with official rules being adopted in 1868, after which the popularity of the sport spread. Ireland soon developed a national team and by the mid-20th century they had won the International Championship (now known as the Six Nations Championship). Ireland has competed in the Rugby World Cup since the first tournament and their best performance to date was in 2011 when they made it to the quarter finals.

IRELAND RUGBY TEAM
Celebrate after winning the 2009 Six Nations Championship.

Russborough House 18th-century house in *County Wicklow*. It is Ireland's longest house, measuring 700 ft (210 m).

Ryanair Low-cost airline based at Dublin Airport. It serves 165 destinations across Europe and North Africa and its success and rapid expansion is due to the deregulation of the aviation industry and its unique business model. *Michael O'Leary* is the CEO of Ryanair and is one of the wealthiest men in Ireland.

RYANAIR
Is one of the most successful low-cost airlines in the world.

S

Sacred The term refers to many of the ancient sites that link Ireland to its very first inhabitants and also refers to places of historic importance or pilgrimage.

Sands, Robert (Bobby) *(1954–1981)* Republican who was an active member of the *Provisional IRA* during the *Troubles*. He was imprisoned for firearms offences and led a prisoner protest demanding political status through means of *hunger strikes*. He was elected to the British Parliament while in jail, and died after 66 days of refusing food.

CROAGH PATRICK
Is one of the most important pilgrimage locations in Ireland.

Sayings There are hundreds of Irish sayings, passed down through the generations.

Examples are:

✦ May the luck of the Irish be with you!

✦ Here's to a long life and a merry one. A quick death and an easy one. A pretty girl and an honest one. A cold pint and another one!

✦ If you're lucky enough to be Irish ... You're lucky enough!

✦ May you have the hindsight to know where you've been, the foresight to know where you are going, and the insight to know when you have gone too far.

Science and Technology Irish scientists have been successful since the 14th century. Some inventions and discoveries are:

✦ Modern chemistry – *Robert Boyle*

✦ The induction coil – *Nicholas Callan*

✦ Seismology – *Robert Mallett*

✦ Submarine – *John Phillip Holland*

✦ Nickel-zinc battery – *Dr James Drumm*

Scott, William *(1913–1989)* Abstract painter well known for his still lifes.

NICKEL-ZINC BATTERIES
Perform well in high-drain applications and are often used in power tools.

SUBMARINE
John Holland devised the first submarine as a way to attack Britain.

Scully, Sean *(1945–)* Irish-born American painter. He has been nominated for a Turner Prize twice and his art appears in museums throughout the world.

SDLP (Social Democratic and Labour Party) Political party in Northern Ireland. It is a Nationalist party, with many of its supporters coming from the Catholic population. Its ultimate aim is for a united Ireland through non-violent, constitutional means. Its current leader is Margaret Ritchie. However, previous leader *John Hume* was instrumental in the peace talks and the *IRA* ceasefire, which culminated in the *Good Friday Agreement*.

Seanad Éireann The upper house of parliament. Membership is elected by a narrow electoral college of vocational and educational interests and nominated by the *Taoiseach*. A government proposal to abolish the Seanad was narrowly defeated in a referendum in 2013.

SEANAD ÉIREANN
The Seanad chamber in Leinster House, Dublin.

Shackleton's Endurance Sir Ernest Shackleton was an Anglo-Irish explorer. In 1914, Shackleton and a crew of 27 set sail for the last unclaimed prize in the history of exploration – the first crossing on foot of the Antarctic continent. Within 85 miles (137 km) of the continent, their ship *Endurance* was trapped and slowly crushed by pack ice. With no communication with the outside world their ordeal lasted 20 months. With Shackleton's leadership, the crew struggled to stay alive in one of the most inhospitable regions of the world. Miraculously, not one man was lost, surviving extreme cold, breaking ice floes, leopard seal attacks and an open boat journey that would later be called one of the greatest navigational feats in nautical history.

ERNEST SHACKLETON
Explorer best remembered for keeping his crew safe during their Antarctic journey.

SHAMROCK
The unofficial emblem of Ireland.

Shamrock The unofficial emblem of Ireland. It is associated with *St Patrick*, who is said to have explained the Holy Trinity using its three leaves.

RIVER SHANNON
The longest river in Ireland.

HANNA SHEEHY-SKEFFINGTON
An ardent campaigner for women's rights.

Shannon, River The longest river in Ireland, it flows through Loughs Allen, Ree and Derg. It is well known for its *salmon fishing* and hydroelectric installation.

Shaw, George Bernard *(1856–1950)* Theatre critic and cofounder of the London School of Economics and very successful dramatist. A socialist, teetotaller, vegetarian and home-ruler, he won the Nobel Prize for Literature in 1925.

Sheehy-Skeffington, Hanna *(1877–1946)* Feminist who campaigned for voting rights for women. She was the founder of the Irish Women Graduates' Association, as well as the Irish Women's Franchise League. She was imprisoned for her protests against the exclusion of women from the *Home Rule* Bill.

Sheela-na-Gig An ancient carving found outside many medieval buildings, depicting a woman exposing enlarged genitalia. Its origins are unknown; some believe it to be pagan, whilst others believe it to be Celtic or even Christian.

Sheridan, Richard Brinsley *(1751–1816)* A dramatist by trade, he preferred politics and became a member of parliament in 1780, serving in many key roles, including that of treasurer to the Navy.

Shipbuilding *Belfast* has always been the centre for Irish shipbuilding, which boomed as an industry during the 19th century. The most famous ship built in Ireland was the *Titanic*.

Sinn Féin Political party founded in 1905 by *Arthur Griffith*. It serves both the Republic of Ireland and Northern Ireland. It was the driving force behind Irish independence during the early 20th century and its stature rose again during the *Troubles*. Sinn Féin's leader, *Gerry Adams*, was instrumental during the peace talks that led to the *Good Friday Agreement*, although some opposed Sinn Féin's involvement because it is the political wing of the *IRA*.

SINN FÉIN
Rose in popularity during the early 20th century.

Siege of Derry *(1689)* A siege during the war between William of Orange and King James II. The city was initially a Protestant stronghold.

Siege of Drogheda *(1649)* The scene of a massacre during *Cromwell*'s invasion; over 2,000 soldiers and 1,000 civilians were killed.

Silken Thomas *(1513–1537)* A prominent figure in Irish *history*. Upon hearing rumours of his father's execution, he revolted against English rule, hoping to attract support from Catholics affected by *Henry VIII's* dissolution of the monasteries. His actions, however, put tighter restrictions in place and led to the creation of the Kingdom of Ireland in 1542.

Skelligs, the A group of islands off the coast of *County Kerry*.

SIEGE OF DROGHEDA
Drogheda was a royalist town with soldiers who had supported Charles I. As a result many soldiers who were murdered after surrender were English and Scottish.

S

Slieve Bloom (**Mountains of Bladhma**)
A mountain range just north of *County Tipperary*. They are named after a Celtic warrior who took refuge in the mountains.

Sligo, County County in the Republic of Ireland on the north-west Atlantic coast. It is the site of many *megaliths* and passage tombs, including *Knocknarea*. The county has a strong association with *W.B. Yeats*, who is buried in Drumcliffe churchyard.

Sligo, town Despite being a seaport town, its main industries are in healthcare and pharmaceutical products. It has the ruins of a 15th-century abbey, and there is a megalithic burial site three miles away at Carrowmore.

Smurfit, Michael (*1936–*) Engineer who built one of the world's largest paper and packaging companies. He was listed 25th on the 2010 *Irish Independent* Rich List. The graduate business school at University College Dublin is named after him.

BEN BULBEN
A famous natural landmark of County Sligo.

MEGALITHIC CEMETERY
County Sligo has many ancient archaeological sites.

Somerville, Edith *(1858–1949)* An Irish novelist based in Castletownbere, County Cork, who wrote stories about Irish life.

Somerville and Ross The joint pseudonym for the writers *Edith Somerville* and Violet Martin. Their collaboration began in 1887 and their best known work is *Some Experiences of an Irish RM* (1889). Somerville continued to write under the joint pseudonym after Martin's death in 1915.

Spanish Armada *(1588)* When the Spanish tried to invade England, their ships were blown off course following their defeat. Storms blew them towards the west coast of Ireland and the British government put in place harsh measures to make sure the Irish did not assist them. Many of the Spanish men were put to death, died at sea or fled to Scotland.

SPANISH ARMADA
Their fate was sealed when strong winds forced them off course.

Spring, Dick (**Richard**) *(1950–)* Businessman and former Labour Party leader. He became Tánaiste (deputy prime minister) in 1982 when Labour and *Fine Gael* formed a coalition government, and held three Ministries: Environment (1982–3), Energy (1983–7) and Foreign Affairs (1994–7).

Sport Ireland is well known for its sporting achievements and participates in many different sports at international level. Ireland also has native sports, the most popular being *hurling*, *camogie* and *Gaelic football*.

Over the years Ireland has produced many sporting stars in various arenas. The most famous sportsmen and women are:

George Best – footballer, Linda Byrne – athlete, Michael Carruth – Olympic boxer, *Ken Doherty* – snooker player, Shay Given – footballer, *Pádraig Harrington* – golfer, *Alex Higgins* – snooker player, *Eddie Irvine* – F1 driver, *Robbie Keane* – footballer, Roy Keane – footballer, Sean Kelly – cyclist, *Michael Kinane* – jockey, *Paul McGrath* – footballer, Brian O'Driscoll – rugby player, Ronan O'Gara – rugby player, Sonia O'Sullivan – athlete, and Nicholas and *Stephen Roche* – cyclists, and *Katie Taylor*, Olympic boxer.

GAELIC FOOTBALL
Is a popular sport
indigenous to Ireland.

RONAN O'GARA
Preparing to take a
penalty kick for Ireland.

Stoker, Bram *(1847–1912)* Novelist most famous for his novel *Dracula* (1897).

Stormont The site of the Northern Ireland Assembly, which was set up following the *Good Friday Agreement* (1998).

TOMB OF STRONGBOW
You can see Strongbow's tomb in Christ Church Cathedral, Dublin.

Strongbow (**Richard de Clare**) *(1130–1176)* He is famous for winning land back from the *Vikings* for king *Dermot MacMurrough*, as leader of the Normans. In return he was given the hand in marriage of the king's daughter, Aoife. Dermot died soon afterwards and was succeeded by Strongbow.

STRONGBOW
Was a Norman invader who won back land from the Vikings.

St Patrick's Day Celebrated internationally on 17 March, it is the feast day of Ireland's patron saint.

Strokestown Park An 18th-century country house built on the site of a 16th-century castle, situated in *County Roscommon*. It is home to the Irish National Famine Museum.

Superstitions The Irish have many superstitions. Some of the most famous are:

✦ If a magpie comes to your door, it's a sure sign of death.

✦ Crowing hens and whistling girls are bad luck.

✦ If your palm itches it means you will come into money.

✦ Evil spirits cannot cross running water.

✦ It is unlucky to ask a man on his way to fish where he is going.

Swift, Jonathan *(1667–1745)* Dean of St Patrick's Cathedral in Dublin, Swift is famous for *Gulliver's Travels* (1726). His work is satirical and often attacks corruption within religious and educational establishments.

BLACK CATS
That cross your path will bring good luck.

JONATHAN SWIFT
He is most famous as the author of *Gulliver's Travels*.

T

TAILTEANN GAMES
Was a serious sporting event
in the early 20th century.

Taaffe, Patrick *(1930–1992)* National hunt jockey who won the Cheltenham Cup three years in a row between 1964 and 1966, and was the first jockey ever to win it four times in 1968.

Tailteann Games A modern revival of ancient games played from around 630 BC. It was presided over by various high kings, including *Brian Boru*. Although the games were revived seriously in the early and mid parts of the 20th century with international athletes taking part, it is now a more casual event and forms part of school athletics.

TAOISIGH OF IRELAND

Name	Terms of Office	Party
Éamon de Valera	1932–1948	Fianna Fáil
John A. Costello	1948–1951	Fine Gael
Éamon de Valera	1951–1954	Fianna Fáil
John A. Costello	1954–1957	Fine Gael
Éamon de Valera	1957–1959	Fianna Fáil
Seán Lemass	1959–1966	Fianna Fáil
Jack Lynch	1966–1973	Fianna Fáil
Liam Cosgrave	1973–1977	Fine Gael
Jack Lynch	1977–1979	Fianna Fáil
Charles Haughey	1979–1981	Fianna Fáil
Garret FitzGerald	1981–1982	Fine Gael
Charles Haughey	1982–1982	Fianna Fáil
Garret FitzGerald	1982–1987	Fine Gael
Charles Haughey	1987–1992	Fianna Fáil
Albert Reynolds	1992–1994	Fianna Fáil
John Bruton	1994–1997	Fine Gael
Bertie Ahern	1997–2008	Fianna Fáil
Brian Cowen	2008–2011	Fianna Fáil
Enda Kenny	2011–	Fine Gael

ENDA KENNY
Became Taoiseach in 2011.

Taoiseach The name given to the prime minister of the Republic of Ireland.

T

Temperance Movement Inspired by prohibition movements in America, Catholics followed the examples of free church organisations and formed the Irish Temperance League in 1858; their aim was to limit the consumption of alcohol in Ireland as the drinking of *whiskey* and *poteen* had become a social problem.

THIN LIZZY
Were extremely successful in the 1970s.

Thin Lizzy Rock band from the 1970s led by *Phil Lynott*. They were one of the first bands from Ireland to achieve international success.

Tipperary, County Situated in *Munster* province it is a popular tourist destination due to its many attractions, which include the *Rock of Cashel* and *Cahir Castle*.

Tipperary, town Probably best known for the song, 'It's a Long Way to Tipperary', which was a popular wartime song in World Wars I and II. It is a market town popular for hiking trails.

Titanic The famous ill-fated ship that struck an iceberg and sank on its maiden voyage. It was built and launched in *Belfast* in 1912. Many lives were lost due to the inadequate number of lifeboats available.

Tithe The term given to a tax levied on crops since the 12th century, which went directly to the Church, latterly to the Protestant Church of Ireland. This was a bone of contention for many Catholic farmers, but it remained in force until the *Disestablishment* of the Church of Ireland in 1869.

Tone, Theobald Wolfe *(1763–1798)* One of the leaders of the *Rebellion of 1798* and a founding member of the *United Irishmen*. He was captured by the British Navy for trying to land French forces and sentenced to death. He committed suicide in prison to avoid a public execution.

TITANIC
It famously sank on its maiden voyage.

WOLFE TONE
Led the rebellion of 1798.

Tourism Ireland is a popular tourist destination. There is a large variety of things to see and do, from its stunning landscapes and coastal scenery to its rich history and heritage, as well as its people and culture. Ireland's *history* dates back as far as 6000 BC and since then a lot has happened, including invasions, battles, *St Patrick* and, of course, the great *diaspora* has meant that Ireland's culture and heritage has spread throughout the world. Wherever you visit in Ireland you will encounter a culture that has developed over thousands of years – there's passion for food, drink, music and dance, and you'll never be far away from a good time. And although Ireland is predominantly rural, there are *cities* and urban hubs that are well worth visiting, including both capital cities: *Belfast* in Northern Ireland and *Dublin* in the Republic of Ireland.

IRISH TOURIST OFFICE
Most towns have their own tourist office with information on local attractions.

There are so many things to see and do in Ireland that you'll be spoiled for choice. There are events running all year round, from sports and festivals to concerts, theatrical performances, workshops, as well as museums, galleries and exhibitions. Wherever you go, you'll be able to experience traditional Irish *food and drink*, go shopping in the market towns or big cities, or even visit a spa. If you're looking for activities, Ireland has mountain ranges for climbing and hiking, as well as unspoiled landscapes in which to enjoy cycling, fishing and horse-riding – and many *beaches* offer water sports during the summer months. As for culture and heritage, Ireland has many castles, monuments and ancient ruins of historical interest and importance; you will even be able to trace your Irish ancestry.

IRELAND'S LANDSCAPE
Is a big draw for tourists visiting Ireland.

Transport Up until the mid 20th century, many Irish people still used horses and traps, as well as canals as their main method of transportation. However, since industrialisation and the economic boom during the 1960s, and later the 1990s, Ireland's transport infrastructure has grown and developed.

✦ *Railways* – Intercity services operate throughout Northern Ireland and the Republic of Ireland; suburban networks also operate in *Belfast* and *Dublin*. There are few lines in the north-west of the island due to Éamon de Valera's decommissioning of them during the 1930s.

✦ *Roads* – Roads in Ireland are designed to link Dublin with all the major cities. The government-run Bus Éireann provides local and inter-city services in the Republic of Ireland, and Ulsterbus provides a similar service in Northern Ireland. Driving in both countries is on the left.

RAILWAYS
Intercity services operate throughout Northern Ireland and the Republic of Ireland.

✦ *Waterways* – Ireland has several inland waterways. Those most used are the *Grand Canal*, Royal Canal and the Shannon-Erne Waterway. Being an island, there are many ports and harbours connecting Ireland to Britain and the rest of Europe.

✦ *Airports* – There are four main airports in the Republic of Ireland, at *Dublin*, *Cork*, Shannon and *Knock*; in Northern Ireland the main airport is Belfast International. Ireland's national airline is *Aer Lingus*, which services many European and transatlantic destinations. In the last decade, *Ryanair's* popularity has boomed with the deregulation of airports and its cheap ticket offers.

FERRIES
Are a popular way of getting to the rest of Europe.

AER LINGUS
Ireland's oldest airline serves many international destinations.

Trimble, David *(1944–)* Former leader of the *UUP* (Ulster Unionist Party); he became Northern Ireland's first minister following the 1998 *Good Friday Agreement*. Later that year, he was awarded the Nobel Peace Prize in recognition of his contribution to the *Northern Ireland Peace Process*.

DAVID TRIMBLE
Contributed to the Northern Ireland Peace Process.

Trinity College Dublin Ireland's oldest university, founded in 1592. It was originally designed to train Protestant clergy and was initially open only to Protestants. Many influential politicians, writers and scientists have studied at Trinity College, including *Henry Grattan*, *Jonathan Swift*, *Samuel Beckett*, *Oscar Wilde* and former Irish president, *Mary McAleese*. The college is recognised as one of the best universities in the world and now promotes equality of access to all. The university offers around 14,000 places per year.

TRINITY COLLEGE DUBLIN
Is recognised as one of the best universities in the world.

Troubles The term used to describe the ongoing violence caused by disagreements between Catholic Nationalists and Protestant Unionists. Although these disagreements stretch back to the time of *Henry VIII*, the term is used to describe the modern period that started in the late 1960s when civil rights movements caused violence to escalate, with both sides using terrorism as a political statement. In an attempt to end the religious discrimination and associated violence in Northern Ireland, the Civil Rights Movement became a spark that unwittingly helped to ignite the Troubles. Some Catholic areas of *Belfast* became off-limits even to police and military. Peace talks and international political intervention eventually led to ceasefires and the *Good Friday Agreement*.

THE GHERKIN, LONDON
Built on the site of the Baltic Exchange, which was destroyed by an IRA bomb in 1992.

TULLAMORE COUNCIL
Meet in this building.

TULLYNALLY CASTLE
The largest occupied country house in Ireland.

Tullamore, town Situated in *County Offaly* on the route of the *Grand Canal*. It is the site of Durrow Abbey, which is said to have been founded by *St Columba (Colum Cille)* in AD 551 and the place where the *Book of Durrow* was written.

Tullynally Castle 17th-century country house in *County Westmeath*. Gothic stylings were added in the early 19th century and it was extended further in 1840. It is the largest occupied country house in Ireland.

Tweed A woven woollen textile that was particularly popular in the late 1800s, when traditional sports and country pursuits became popular with the upper classes. Tweed has been produced in the northern counties of Ireland, primarily Donegal and Tyrone, for many generations. Irish tweed is known for its use of natural colours, derived from dyes made from flowers and berries.

Tyndall, John *(1820–1893)* A prominent physicist who is famous for explaining why the sky is blue. The Tyndall Effect, which describes how invisible particles affect the way light scatters, is named after him. It is used today to determine the density of particles in aerosol sprays. He published 17 books during his career and was appointed professor of physics at the Royal Institution in London. Tyndall was also one the first physicists to prove that the greenhouse effect existed.

Tyrone, County One of the six counties of Northern Ireland; its chief town is *Omagh*. The county lies on the borders of *Lough Neagh* and is the site of many Neolithic graves and stone circles. The name Tyrone is derived from the old Irish, Tír Eoghain, which means 'land of Eoghan'. The Eoghan referred to was, most probably, the son of King Niall. As the English settled in Northern Ireland, the name became anglicised to Tyrowen and later, Tyrone.

JOHN TYNDALL
Best known for explaining why the sky is blue.

COAT OF ARMS
For County Tyrone is derived from the arms of King Niall.

U

U2
Performing in Cardiff
during their *Vertigo* tour.

U2 Ireland's most successful rock group and one of the most successful bands of the 1980s and 1990s. The band's members are: *Bono*, 'The Edge', Adam Clayton and Larry Mullen Jr. The strong political messages in their first album, particularly in the song 'Sunday, Bloody Sunday', paved the way for future charity events, including *Beb Geldof*'s Live Aid and Band Aid ventures. They have a huge following and the 360° Tour (2009–12) was the largest grossing tour of all time, beating the Rolling Stones' record for the Bigger Bang Tour. *Rolling Stone* magazine ranked U2 as number 22 in the list of the '100 Greatest Artists Of All Time'.

Ulster Province in the north of Ireland, which has been the central place of Scottish and English settlements. The majority of Ulster lies in Northern Ireland and consists of the counties of *Antrim*, *Armagh*, *Down*, *Fermanagh*, *Derry* and *Tyrone*; the remainder lies in the Republic of Ireland and consists of the counties of *Cavan*, *Donegal* and *Monaghan*.

Ulster Plantation *(1609)* The term given to the resettlement of counties in *Ulster* by the English, implemented by the English government. The division and confiscation of land led to many disputes between settlers and native freeholders, who lost many of their rights. The Ulster Plantation is seen by many as the origin of the sectarian problems in Northern Ireland.

THE ULSTER PLANTATION
Saw many native Irish expelled from their homes and their land.

UDA MURAL
In Waterside, Derry.

UVF MURAL
The UVF was a Protestant
terrorist organisation.

UDA (**Ulster Defence Association**) A loyalist paramilitary group set up in 1971 to defend loyalist areas from violent Irish Republicanism. They also used the name UFF (Ulster Freedom Fighters) to claim responsibility for terrorist attacks.

UTV (**Ulster Television**) Branch of ITV, broadcasting independent television in Northern Ireland.

UUP (**Ulster Unionist Party**) The second largest political party in Northern Ireland, it promotes equality for Northern Ireland within the UK and opposes a union with the Republic of Ireland. Its former leader, *David Trimble*, became the first minister in 1998 following the *Good Friday Agreement*.

UVF (**Ulster Volunteer Force**) A loyalist paramilitary group that was particularly active during the *Troubles* of the 1960s and 1970s through to the early 1990s. They signed a ceasefire in 1994.

Undertones Punk rock band from Northern Ireland led by Feargal Sharkey (who was later replaced by Paul McLoone). Their most famous song was 'Teenage Kicks' from 1978.

Union, Act of *(1801)* Act passed by both the British and Irish parliaments; it brought Ireland into the United Kingdom. It was most likely triggered by the *Rebellion of 1798*, which showed the danger of divided authority. The act was opposed by many. Many Catholics opposed the union and fought continually for *Home Rule*, which eventually led to the creation of the Free State.

United Irishmen Society formed in 1791 by *Wolfe Tone*. Its aim was to campaign for parliamentary reform and Catholic emancipation. They supported, and were influenced by, the French Revolution, and sought help from the French military to aid what eventually became the *Rebellion of 1798*.

DAMIAN O'NEILL
Of the Undertones – pictured here in 2007.

V

Valentia A small island off the coast of *County Kerry*. As well as being the site of many medieval ruins, it was a terminal station for the first ever transatlantic cable.

Vikings The Vikings, who were seafaring warriors from Scandanavia, began to attack Ireland at the end of the 8th century. At first they penetrated only the offshore islands, but by the mid 9th century they had moved further inland and had begun to build settlements, soon becoming part of the Irish political landscape. *Brian Boru* finally defeated the Vikings at the *Battle of Clontarf*, which ended their control of *Dublin*, and they eventually became integrated into Irish society.

VIKINGS
Began to invade Ireland during the 8th century.

W

Walsh, Louis *(1952–)* Music manager who has managed several Irish acts, including *Boyzone*, *Westlife* and *Jedward*. He is most well known as a judge on the TV show *The X Factor*.

Walton, Conor *(1970–)* Artist who is known for his very realistic still-life paintings. He has won many awards for his portraits and has hosted several solo exhibitions.

War of Independence *(1919–21)* War fought between the *IRA* and the British armed forces. It was triggered by the assassination of two policemen in *Tipperary* by the *IRA*. A truce was eventually called in 1921, when peace talks led to the *Anglo-Irish Treaty*.

LOUIS WALSH
He is most famous for his role as a judge on *The X Factor*.

Waterford, County Situated in the south of the Republic of Ireland, it features *Lismore Castle* and the *Knockmealdown Mountains*, and the coastline (the Copper Coast) has been designated a UNESCO geopark.

Waterford, town A harbour town situated on the River Suir and on the Atlantic Coast. Waterford was an important Norman stronghold and was noted for its loyalty to Britain.

WESTLIFE
Are Ireland's most successful boy band.

Westlife Boy band established in 1998. They were originally signed by Simon Cowell and are now managed by *Louis Walsh*. They have achieved great success, particularly in the UK, and hold the record for the greatest number of consecutive number ones.

Westmeath, County Situated in the province of *Leinster*, it is a popular location for *fishing* and its land is used for cattle and dairy farming. The county also contains many ancient monuments and historical remains.

Westport, town A market town in *County Mayo*. Its most notable landmark is *Croagh Patrick*, a pilgrimage site in July every year.

WESTPORT HOUSE
A Georgian mansion popular with tourists.

Westport House A Georgian mansion situated near the coast of Clew Bay in *County Mayo*.

Wexford, County One of the most farmed counties in the Republic of Ireland, its main crops are wheat, barley, beet and potatoes. It also has a strong *fishing* industry and has a large fishing port at Kilmore Quay. The *John F. Kennedy Arboretum* is one of the most popular tourist attractions in the county.

Wexford, town A seaport in *County Wexford*, it has been the scene of many battles, including *Viking* invasions, Norman conquests, *Cromwell*'s siege and the *Rebellion of 1798*, possibly due to its strategic location.

Weather There is a joke in Ireland that the way to tell the difference between summer and winter is the temperature of the rain! The climate in Ireland is temperate despite its northerly geographical location – this is due to warm currents from the North Atlantic Drift (Gulf Stream). June, July and August are the warmest months of the year, whilst January and February are the coldest. Ireland doesn't often experience extreme weather, but it has been known to snow and reach freezing temperatures in the winter. It is advisable to take a raincoat with you, even at the height of summer. Many Irish people swim in the sea all year round, particularly on Christmas Day.

RAINBOWS
Are common in Ireland due to the high rainfall. Legend has it that a crock, or pot, of gold can be found at the end of the rainbow and leprechauns can tell you where exactly this might be.

Whelan, Bill *(1950–)* Composer best known for writing the music for *Riverdance*, which was first performed at the *Eurovision Song Contest* in 1994. The music was released as a single in the UK and reached number nine.

Whiskey, Irish An alcoholic spirit made from fermented grains and distilled in wooden casks. Irish whiskey is distilled three times and, unlike Scottish whiskey, does not use peat in the production, which gives it a sweeter taste. There are many Irish distilleries, based mainly in the counties of *Dublin*, *Belfast* and *Cork*, the most famous being Jameson.

White Island An island off the eastern shore of *Lough Erne* in *County Fermanagh*. Features include a ruined church with an intact Romanesque archway, and eight carved figures dating from AD 800–1000, one of which is presumed to be a *Sheela na Gig*. The island is accessed by ferry from Castle Archdale Country Park.

JAMESON WHISKEY
Is one of Ireland's best-known exports.

POWERSCOURT WATERFALL
In County Wicklow is the
tallest waterfall in Ireland.

Wicklow, County A picturesque coastal county in Leinster, Wicklow is known as the Garden of Ireland. It is famous for its mountain walks.

Wicklow, town Town south-east of Dublin, it forms a rough semicircle around Wicklow harbour.

Workhouses Following the *Act of Union* in 1801, the English addressed the widespread problem of poverty in Ireland. In 1838 the Irish Poor Law was passed, which was very similar to the English Poor Law of 1834. The workhouse system was part of the law and its objective was to help those in extreme poverty by offering them accommodation and employment. Life in a workhouse was deliberately harsh in order to deter the masses, so that only the truly destitute would apply. During *The Great Famine*, workhouses became overwhelmed with those starving and impoverished; this led to assisted emigration.

W

Wilde, Oscar *(1854–1900)* Flamboyant writer and poet who became heavily involved in London society. He studied at *Trinity College Dublin* before moving to London where he was a journalist. He became well known for his wit, eccentric dress and personality. His only novel, *The Picture of Dorian Gray,* was published in 1890 and he then went on to write several plays, his most famous being *The Importance of Being Earnest* (1895) and *Lady Windermere's Fan* (1892).

Though married, he was homosexual, and was the lover of Lord Alfred Douglas. Douglas' father provoked Wilde into suing him, which led to Wilde's financial ruin and imprisonment. Whilst in prison he wrote *The Ballad of Reading Gaol* and a letter, *De Profundis*, which explained his side of the relationship. After his release, he was reunited with Douglas, despite disapproval from both of their families. He died in exile in Paris.

OSCAR WILDE
Died in exile, aged 46.

STATUE OF JUSTICE
Outside Dublin Castle.

'X' Case 1992 court case. A 14-year-old girl who had been raped and became pregnant was refused permission, through an injunction, to leave the Republic of Ireland in order to obtain an abortion. Because the girl was already in England, her parents faced a fine or imprisonment if they did not secure her return. The injunction failed after a Supreme Court ruling allowed her to travel. The case prompted referendums and an investigation into human rights in Ireland. Abortion remains illegal in the Republic of Ireland despite only a minority of the population believing it to be unacceptable in any circumstance.

Young Ireland The term given to social, political and cultural movements during the mid 19th century, which influenced changes in Irish Nationalism. It was originally a negative term used to describe people who campaigned for the repeal of the *Act of Union*. In 1848, ringleaders who planned a failed rebellion were captured and sentenced to death; however, public sympathy encouraged the British government to change their sentence and they were exiled to Van Diemen's Land (Tasmania).

YOUNG IRELAND
Print shows Lord Chief Justice Doherty, standing (left), imposing a death sentence on members of the rebel group, Young Ireland, standing (right).

W. B. YEATS
Is widely regarded as
Ireland's greatest poet.

Yeats, Jack Butler *(1871–1957)* One of Ireland's most famous painters. He started as an illustrator, but quickly moved on to oil paintings. His expressionist style depicted Irish life and landscapes at the time. He is the brother of *W. B. Yeats*, and although born into a Protestant family, he identified with Republican ideals.

Yeats, W(illiam) B(utler) *(1865–1939)* Poet and playwright who was the leader of the Irish literary revival. He was also a founder of the *Abbey Theatre*. He is often remembered for his romantic and lyric poems, many of which were addressed to his unrequited love, *Maud Gonne*. He was an active campaigner for Irish *literature* and several of his works drew heavily on Irish *mythology*. He won the Nobel Prize for Literature in 1923. In his later years, he also served as an Irish senator for two terms, and advocated divorce against strong Catholic opposition at that time.

Z

Zoo, Dublin Located in Phoenix Park, it is the largest zoo in Ireland and one of Dublin's most popular attractions; it was first opened in 1831. It works together with other international zoos to help conserve endangered species. The zoo is split into distinctive areas, namely: World of Cats, World of Primates, The Kazaringa Forest Trail, Fringes of the Arctic, African Plains, Birds, Reptiles, Plants, City Farm and Endangered Species.

DUBLIN ZOO
Is home to 600 animals.

Acknowledgments

Picture credits

Cover: Wikipedia, Pawel Gaul / Photos.com, Meldayus / Photos.com, TPL, Philippa Banks / Photos.com, D. Shankbone / Wikipedia, Sean O'Connor / Wikipedia, Harry Potts / Flickr, Jupiter Images, NASA, www.gaaboard.com, Lisa Valder / Photos.com, John Wilson / Photos.com, Stockbyte, Barbara Hodges

Photos.com: pp.11, 12, 14, 16, 17, 21, 22, 24, 28, 30, 32, 36, 38, 40, 42, 44, 45, 46, 47, 51, 52, 53, 57, 61, 66, 70, 72, 75, 76, 80, 84, 85, 86 (bl), 87, 93, 97, 99, 100, 102, 103, 104, 107, 108, 111, 112, 113, 118 (bl), 120, 124, 128, 130, 133, 135, 147, 149 (br),150 (br), 151 (tr), 152, 153, 155, 158, 163, 165, 168, 172, 173 (br), 174, 175, 176 (all), 177 (br), 178, 181, 183, 184, 185, 191 (br), 192, 198, 209 (br), 210, 211, 213 (br), 214, 215 (br), 216, 217, 220 (tl), 223, 227 (tr), 232, 233, 234, 236 (br), 247, 248, 250, 251 (tr), 252, 255

Wikipedia: pp.25, 26, 29, 37, 39, 41, 43, 49, 54, 56 (bl), 58, 63, 64, 73, 88, 105, 109, 110, 115 (tr), 116, 117, 118 (tl), 121, 122, 123, 131, 132, 136, 137 (bl), 138, 142, 143, 144, 146, 148, 149 (tr), 150 (tr), 154, 157, 159, 161, 167, 169, 171, 172, 173 (tr), 177 (tr), 182, 186 (bl), 187 (tr), 188, 189,190, 193, 194, 196 (bl), 197, 201, 202, 204, 205, 206, 207, 208, 209 (tr), 213 (tr), 215 (tr), 218, 221, 224, 225, 229, 230, 232-233, 235, 236 (tr), 237, 238, 239, 240, 242 (tl), 243, 245, 246, 249, 251 (br), 253, 254

TPL: pp.13, 15, 18, 19, 20, 21, 23, 27, 31, 33, 34, 35, 50, 55, 59, 65, 67, 68-69, 77, 79, 86 (tl), 89, 90, 91, 92, 95, 98, 101, 115 (br), 125, 126, 129, 137 (tl), 141, 145, 156, 162, 164, 180, 186 (tl), 187 (br), 191 (tr), 195, 196 (tl), 200 (bl), 219, 222, 226, 231, 241 242 (bl), 244

Shutterstock: p.102 Bouchan

Michael Diggin: pp. 62, 151 (br), 160

Library Of Congress: pp. 78, 82, 83 (tl), 96, 114, 139, 166, 227 (br)

George P. Landon, victorianweb.org: p131

iStockphoto.com: pp.18, 47

Fáilte Ireland: p.60

Andrew Bowden/Flickr: p.140

Simon Carrasco/Flickr: p.199

Antonio Abrignani/Shutterstock: p.83 (bl)

Peter Plehov: p.94

NGI/Walter Osborne (1859–1903): p.134

NYPL Digital Gallery: p.192

www.gaaboard.com: p.228

Illustrations by: Anthony Morris, Kay Dixey, Gilly Marklew, Peter Bull Studios, Jacqueline East, Mike Spoor

Every effort has been made to trace copyright holders not mentioned here. If there have been any omissions, we will be happy to rectify this in a reprint.